BE QUICK
TO LISTEN

Practice the Spiritual Discipline of
Christian-Listening

RICK BOMMELJE and
CHRISTINE T. WETHMAN

BE QUICK TO LISTEN
Practice the Spiritual Discipline of Christian-Listening

ISBN 10:1548109819
ISBN 13:978-1548109813

Library of Congress Control Number: 2018944188
Printed in the United States of America
CreateSpace
First Printing: 2018

Published by:

A non-profit organization to help the world listen better.
To order, visit www.bequicktolisten.com

DEDICATION

We dedicate this book to Christians worldwide, and seekers of the Christian faith, who commit to practice the spiritual discipline of listening to 'be quick to listen' to God and make a glorious difference in their lives and the lives of others.

CONTENTS

ACKNOWLEDGEMENTS

Be Quick to Listen has been an outgrowth of decades of Divine inspiration on the significance that listening plays in the scriptures as a spiritual discipline.

We are grateful to the Reverend Dr. Wally Arp, Senior Pastor of St. Luke's Lutheran Church and School, who created the opportunity for us to develop and present a Bible study on listening at St. Luke's. The Bible study became the foundation for *Be Quick to Listen.*

We are thankful to the eight pastors who shared their insights and perspectives with us on Christian-Listening and the importance it plays in their congregations and their personal lives: Reverend Dr. Wally Arp; Reverend Dr. Bob Bushong; Rev. Bryan Chestnutt; Reverend Dr. Bob Henry; Pastor Joel Carl Hunter; Pastor Douglas Neiner; Pastor Tim DeTellis; and Reverend Dr. Debbie Stanley.

We are indebted to Dr. Lyman (Manny) K. Steil, founder of the International Listening Association and one of the foremost authorities on listening in the world. Manny's wisdom has been the foundation for the Listening Knowledge included in *Be Quick to Listen.*

We are grateful to our readers: J.B. Adams, Theresa Campbell, Dr. Sam Certo, Carl Chauncey, Frank Hagy, Wini Hagy, Ixchell Duarte, Shannon Matthews, Denise Messineo, Melody Montgomery, Patricia A. McLeod, Pastor Douglas Neiner, Armando Payas Jr., Kay Lindahl, Dr. Lyman (Manny) Steil, Jan Timbrook, and Dr. Charles Veentra. They provided invaluable feedback to us after reading one of the many drafts. Their perspectives enabled us to re-direct the work into a more compelling creation.

We are appreciative of our editor, Karen Steinmann, whose experience and insight profoundly moved our work forward, and our proofreader, Julie Joyce.

We are thankful to our spouses, Quin Bommelje and Joe Wethman, for their support and encouragement throughout the journey of the creation of *Be Quick to Listen*.

Finally, and most importantly, all of the glory goes to God, Who has blessed us with the incredible opportunity to serve His Kingdom.

INTRODUCTION

"Let the wise listen, and add to their learning, and let the discerning get guidance." Proverbs 1:5 (NIV)

Listening. . . It's the one activity you do more than any other in life except for breathing. Yet, then why are so many facets of listening often misunderstood, forgotten, or ignored? In today's world, it seems a great deal of attention is placed on speaking, while listening rarely receives any fanfare.

Turning a deaf ear to the available wisdom, knowledge, and education about listening often leads to damaged or broken relationships—as well as a loss of love, trust, respect, and credibility. These entail only a few of the costs associated with our inability to listen well. Sometimes, lives are at stake—both physical and spiritual.

Out of His goodness and mercy, God has lifted up listening as a spiritual discipline for Christians to live by and enjoy. To underscore its importance and stress its significance, God gives us more than 2,000 scripture verses that include the words *listen, listening, hear,* and *hearing*—depending upon the Bible translation. Let there be no doubt that God's Word is sending a strong message—BE QUICK TO LISTEN!

THE POWER OF THE HYPHEN IN CHRISTIAN-LISTENING

There is a difference between *Christian Listening* and *Christian-Listening*. The hyphen serves to contrast two approaches to listening. In the unhyphenated version, there is no primacy, whereas in the hyphenated version, this shows that the two words are inseparable. Plainly put, the call for action is to listen to God as you listen to life and respond appropriately. This is a special type of listening that requires a practiced spiritual discipline. Throughout this book, the hyphen will be used in Christian-Listening and Christian-listener.

The purpose of this book is to offer you practical steps on how to listen better to God, to yourself, and to others, all in ways that will enrich your life and strengthen your faith. For every Christian, listening is essential to living an abundant life in Christ.

The unique approach embraced by *BE QUICK TO LISTEN* is based on forging connections between God's Word and formal listening education. This book contains six "Building Blocks" that combine to offer a practice of Christian-Listening. In addition to providing carefully selected scripture verses and Bible applications, each chapter contains a perspective from a Christian leader who practices the spiritual discipline of listening and shares the importance of listening with the faith community.

For example, Reverend Dr. Bob Bushong, is a Methodist pastor for more than 30 years and currently a District Superintendent of the United Methodist Church in Florida.

He stated, *"There are lots of ways to engage in listening to God. This happens through reading scripture, silent meditation, and a focus on what some would call a 'mantra,' or a phrase that one brings to mind. Years ago, during a women's Bible study, one group member who was a stay-at-home mom at the time said that when she did laundry and ironed, she focused her thoughts on whomever she was attending to and paid attention to what came to mind for her during that time. That was a moving statement to me about listening to God even in the midst of the drudgery of folding laundry or ironing. How we go about listening to other people is hard work. It's about taking it all in and really listening to what others are saying, and then responding. It's about focusing."*

Within each Building Block, you'll find an insightful Listening Knowledge lesson following by a real-life example in a Life Application. The following provides an example of a common listening Life Application experience in today's world:

Olivia was annoyed with the wild scene unfolding on the TV screen before her as she watched her favorite news program. The members of the panel being interviewed were simultaneously shouting at and over each other. With the rising tension and growing hostility, the moderator quickly cut to a commercial.

Something seemed hauntingly familiar to Olivia about what she had just witnessed. Her thoughts returned to the discussion of a controversial topic at last week's church council meeting; she saw a striking similarity between the two scenes. At the meeting, one person had been speaking over the other, with raised voices and outward signs of total disrespect. Olivia could also recognize the same pattern happening in her own family. The last holiday get-together wound up being a disaster of hurt feelings because no one was listening.

After a real-world example like this, a valuable debriefing section helps you analyze the learning points before a *Call* for Action challenges and invites you to learn by doing. The result is a stronger understanding of listening as an activity, so central to a deep-rooted relationship with Christ.

For a quick overview of each chapter, the Six Building Blocks[1] of Christian-Listening are as follows:

Building Block #1:   Build a Solid Foundation
This chapter sets the stage for effective Christian-Listening by introducing the SIER* model.

Building Block #2:   Develop Healthy Habits
The focus of this chapter is exploring the 10 positive, healthy listening habits.

Building Block #3:   Take 100% Responsibility
You learn the five purposes of communication and the central role that listening plays in each of them.

Building Block #4: Ditch the Distractions

In this chapter, you discover the different types of distractions, the five attention patterns, and the "myth" of multitasking.

Building Block #5: Lead Your Emotions

This chapter acquaints you with your emotional triggers, suggests three strategies for leading your emotions, and emphasizes the Golden Pause.

Building Block #6: Take Meaningful Action

As an important wrap-up to your learning experience, you discover a 5-stage process for deeply listening to God, yourself, and others.

As you become familiar with the Building Blocks, it's important to remember how they help you lay a solid foundation of listening skills:

- ✧ **Learnable:** They are simple to understand and, with study and application, can be learned in a short period of time.

- ✧ **Practical:** They can be applied anywhere, anytime, with anyone, in any culture, and in all areas of your life.

- ✧ **Invaluable:** As you practice them with consistency, you will reap an abundant harvest of blessings.

- ✧ **Teachable:** They can be easily shared with others.

BE QUICK TO LISTEN emphasizes that listening is one of several spiritual disciplines, an act of love for God, and an important way to extend love to others. Throughout the lessons, your relationship with God will be nurtured and strengthened as you learn to regularly listen to His Word and take appropriate action; you'll discover unlimited opportunities every day to share God's grace and unconditional love with others through deep listening. Heightened awareness and practice of Christian-Listening skills have unlimited potential to impact your life for Christ.

CLOSING PRAYER

Heavenly Father, thank You for the spiritual discipline of listening. When I call out to You, I know You are deeply listening and I am grateful for You. Help me to nurture this life-giving practice in all areas of my life that I may serve Your purposes and be pleasing to You. Guide my thoughts, words, and actions and make me mindful of those in need of a listening ear and the hope of Your presence. Guide me to listen to You as I listen to life and to respond appropriately. In Jesus' name I pray, Amen.

BUILD A SOLID FOUNDATION

"Therefore, everyone who hears these words of mine and puts them into practice is like a wise man who built his house on the rock." **Matthew 7:24 (NIV)**

The first building block of *BE QUICK TO LISTEN* is Build a Solid Foundation. When constructing a building, the quality of the foundation determines the strength and stability of the structure. For the Christian, the Bible is the one true standard—the foundation upon which a life of faith, rooted in Christ, is lived. A believer builds faith in God, thereby nurturing and strengthening a relationship with Christ, by studying and meditating on scripture. In the central scripture verse for the first Building Block, the emphasis is placed on the value and importance of securing a solid foundation.

In one of His parables from the Sermon on the Mount, Jesus uses a simple story to communicate His point to those listening: the only way to build a strong foundation is by obeying His words. As soon as He introduces the word "therefore," the listeners should take heed of what follows: it's Jesus' way of saying that, in light of everything else just shared, here's what you need to do. By including the word "everyone" in this passage, Jesus reveals that His words are intended for all people.

From the beginning, Jesus states that you must *hear* His words. To do so, you must expose yourself to His words of

Truth. You can do this by studying the Bible, reading Christian books, attending worship, getting involved in classes and small groups in your faith community, and regularly meeting with Christian friends who can join you in reading, sharing, and applying God's Word.

Jesus urges you to hear His words, but He doesn't stop there; and neither should you. Hearing His words is not enough. He goes on to say that you must act upon His words—you must actually DO what Jesus wants you to do. You are building your life and strengthening your faith on His words as you obey them.

Christian-Listening means that your listening is deeper, with an added dimension that's absent from typical listening abilities. For believers, a two-way connection is established between God and you. He speaks, and you listen; you speak and He listens. The solid foundation of a spiritual life vibrates through Christian-Listening and inspires the believer to take appropriate action.

When God speaks, He changes people from becoming observers to becoming participants. When people deeply listen to the Word of God, interesting and sometimes amazing things happen. The goal is that Christian-Listening will bring about a transformation—a new way of living.

The most crucial action you must take is to immerse yourself in the Bible and study what it says about listening. Discern how fundamental it is, not only to your faith but to everything you experience, as your faith fills every part of your life.

BIBLE APPLICATION:
JESUS CALLING THE DISCIPLES

In Matthew 4:18-20, Jesus calls the disciples and offers a perfect example of how people who listen to His words are transformed.

"Now, as Jesus was walking by the Sea of Galilee, He saw two brothers, Simon who was called Peter and Andrew, his brother, casting a net into the sea, for they were fishermen. And He said to them, "Follow Me, and I will make you fishers of men." Immediately they left their nets and followed Him."

"Immediately they left their nets and followed Him."

Two brothers named Simon (called Peter) and Andrew know firsthand what it means to enter into a relationship with the Son of God. While walking beside the Sea of Galilee, Jesus signals for these two fishermen to follow Him. They deeply listen to God's call, quickly leave their nets, and follow Him at once. Jesus speaks words, and the disciples take action. They are called, inspired to act, and willingly put their lives on the line, all affected by Christian-Listening.

In Luke 5:1-11, we see the remarkable results that come from listening to Jesus:

One day as Jesus was standing by the Lake of Gennesaret, the people were crowding around Him and listening to the Word of God. He saw at the water's edge two boats left there by the fishermen, who were washing their nets. He got into one of the boats, the one belonging to Simon, and asked him to put out a little from shore. Then He sat down and taught the people from the boat.

When He had finished speaking, He said to Simon, "Put out into deep water, and let down the nets for a catch."

Simon answered, "Master, we've worked hard all night and haven't caught anything. But because You say so, I will let down the nets."

When they had done so, they caught such a large number of fish that their nets began to break. So, they signaled their partners in the other boat to come and help them, and they came and filled both boats so full that they began to sink.

When Simon Peter saw this, he fell at Jesus' knees and said, "Go away from me, Lord; I am a sinful man!" For he and all his companions were astonished at the catch of fish they had taken, and so were James and John, the sons of Zebedee, Simon's partners.

Then Jesus said to Simon, "Don't be afraid; from now on you will fish for people." So, they pulled their boats up on shore, left everything and followed him.

At first it may seem like letting down nets is a small, routine task performed by fishermen, day in and day out. Yet, it's during those boring times that a remarkable transformation happens, and we see that with these men. They can ignore Jesus and what He says, but they listen instead. Jesus speaks and asks them to go fishing in the middle of deep water. True to form, what Jesus says doesn't always make sense to us. And back then, it doesn't make sense to the fishermen either. They can tell Him they aren't going to follow Him, but instead, they listen. Even some skeptical listening is still obedience. It's still listening, and their boats are filled to the brim—to the point of sinking.

The two-part step of listening and taking meaningful action is a foundation of life itself. The listening that goes on between you and God and between you and others is an amazing gift from God. Through listening in our homes, jobs, and relationships with family and friends, we receive God's best for us; it's the way God works. God speaks to us and we listen. With faith in God, there is a profound depth and dimension to listening. It's listening like you've never experienced before.

PASTOR'S LISTENING PERSPECTIVE

Pastor Douglas Neiner is Senior Pastor at Cornerstone Baptist Church in Pittsfield, Massachusetts. He has included Christian-Listening as a central part of his ministry for 40 years.

To me, Christian-Listening is the process of receiving, constructing meaning from, and responding <u>appropriately</u> to spoken and/or non-verbal messages. I include "appropriately" because, oftentimes, people listen and respond, but they're not responding appropriately because they didn't listen properly.

I will give you a personal example. There was a time when I had to take my car to the shop, and I had to ask my wife to come and pick me up with the second car. She asked, "How do I get there?" I said, "You come out of the parking lot and go north on Route 132." This was in northeast Philadelphia at the time. And so, we're talking, and she said, "Is that right or left?" I said, "Honey, you just go out and turn north."

She didn't know where north was, and I did. So, 20 minutes later she still hadn't shown up at the shop. Finally, she came all teary-eyed, and here I thought I'd communicated the directions appropriately, but I hadn't.

Though I thought we communicated, she didn't act appropriately because she didn't understand what I was trying to tell her. I've seen that often with people talking about the same thing and walking away, and then each one doing the complete opposite of what the other person thought they should do. I read an article that described hooks in the back of your brain and how we listen long enough to hang what we hear on a hook, and then we stop listening.

Oftentimes, we hang it on the wrong hook because we didn't listen to the whole conversation in the first place. So, we walk away thinking we understood, and yet we walk away misinformed because we hung it on the wrong hook.

When I think about Christian-Listening, the Bible verse that stands out in my mind is Romans 10:17, "So then faith cometh by hearing; hearing by the Word of God." That's what really got me interested in listening way back in 1978. My dad had given me a tape by Dr. Ralph Nichols, Father of the Field of Listening, with a talk titled, "Listening Is Good Business." Nichols mentions that we only operate on about a 25% efficiency level in listening. At the time, I was in seminary, and I said, "If I can increase my congregation's efficiency in listening, it would have a profound effect on their spiritual growth."

So, if faith cometh by hearing, and hearing by the Word of God, and we're only operating on a 25% efficiency level, if I could increase that, then it would exponentially affect their spiritual growth. I was teaching as an assistant pastor at that time and also teaching in a Christian school, trying to pass that on, and I've been trying to do that ever since.

Another Christian-Listening Scripture verse for me is Psalm 85:8, "I will hear what the Lord will speak, for He will speak peace unto His people and to His saints. But let them not turn again to folly." That shows an attitude that a sinner should take in the presence of a Divine revelation.

For my congregation members, I encourage them to listen to the full conversation before responding. Ephesians 4:29 says, "Let no corrupt communication proceed out of your mouth but that which is to use for edifying, that it may minister grace to the hearer." So, manage how you speak and not try to engage in heated arguments. For graduation, I give every high school senior who I have contact with, whether in our church or through friends, a laminated card listing the 10 Worst Listening Habits and how to overcome them. I cut it down so it's only maybe about 4"x5".

The 10 Worst Listening Habits

1. Calling the subject uninteresting

2. Criticizing the speaker's delivery

3. Getting over-stimulated

4. Listening only for facts

5. Making an outline of everything we hear

6. Faking attention to the speaker

7. Tolerating or creating distractions

8. Evading difficult material

9. Letting emotion-laden words get between us and the speaker

10. Wasting the differential between speech speed and thought speed

---

The reason I laminate it for these kids, especially the ones going off to college, is that I encourage them to carry that with them to each class and refer to it. I laminate it so it can last.

In today's fast-paced world, I encourage people to stay focused on God's Word, rather than being driven by cultural change. It is also important to listen patiently to millennials and their relative mindset and then point them to the Rock of Christ in His Word. I think we sometimes hesitate to give this young mindset guidance because they often throw out all the landmarks of past generations and feel that they're blazing a new trail kind of thing. Let them voice what they have to say without us having to interrupt, get frustrated, or disgusted.

If a Christian is listening well, one would see spiritual growth and maturity in their lives, such as displaying stability in a crisis as a result of listening to and then being anchored to God's Word. You would also see improvement in relationships and greater communication between husband and wife if one or both were to learn to listen better. Between a parent and child, I think it would also have a positive effect.

I personally am an impatient listener, and I think part of that is my role as a fixer—as a husband and as a pastor. As I'm listening, I'm listening through that filter, and I have to fight that because as soon as my wife starts to express a concern, she may only want cathartic listening. She only may want to be able to speak it out. She doesn't want an answer. I'm always ready to give her the answer. I often find at that point I offend her. She's saying, "You're not listening to me." There's no greater insult for me. She knows that it's my hot button since I've been studying this for such a long time. I should be a good listener, but I'm not oftentimes. What I'm trying to do is work to slow down and control my tendency to answer quickly, or think I know the answer, until she's all said and done and then ask her, "What would you like me to do?" as opposed to just giving her the advice I think she needs.

I remember just recently visiting my daughter in North Carolina, and we went out to a Chick-fil-A. I guess only about eight people were in the whole restaurant at that time. There were five sitting at one table, and all five of them had their cell phones out, not talking to each other. They may have been texting each other, I don't know. I'm sitting there amazed, looking at very little conversation going on, and everybody having their cell phones out. I find that to be a distraction.

The internet is also a distraction. Why do I need to listen to you when I can find the answer myself? From a pastor's standpoint, with my charge as an under-shepherd to feed the flock of which the Lord has given me oversight, and then to have to give an account as one that cares for their soul, I find it very difficult to try to compete with all of the national and international speakers I'm being compared to.

So, I think from inside a local church setting, the internet is a great distraction to people. If they don't hear what I have to say, they can always listen to a message online.

While doing some research, I came across an article written in 1914 by George Matthew Adams, and it's called "Listen." It was published in the Daily Evening Journal, *Pittsfield, Massachusetts, on Thursday, August 20, 1914:*

"Listen" by George Matthew Adams[2]

*The wisest man that you ever
talked to was not only a good
reader but a mighty good listener.*
LISTEN
*Don't get the habit that so
many have of getting restless as
soon as somebody begins to talk
to you.*
LISTEN
*The chances are that you will
learn something you did not know.
And don't forget that everybody
has something and knows something that you do not.*
LISTEN
*Half the blunders of this world
are made because people don't
listen to instructions and do not
listen when they have the chance.
Accuracy and speed accumulate to*

the listener.
LISTEN
*And remember that people are
not the only creatures that say
things. There are "signs" in the
very air and at every stage of your
life history, and if you listen you
are liable to hear something that
may prove very important to your
success as well as to your happiness.
So,* LISTEN.

LISTENING KNOWLEDGE

To BE QUICK TO LISTEN, it's important to have a foundation of listening knowledge. Following are some important facts to know:

1. Researchers estimate that approximately 80% of your waking day is spent communicating in one form or another.

2. Of the four communication types (reading, writing, speaking, and listening), at least 45% of that time is spent listening.

3. Listening is the one activity you do more in life than any other, except breathing. It forms the cornerstone of all human behavior.

4. Less than 10% of adults have received formal listening education.

The "Christian-Listening Wisdom" Triangle

The "Christian-Listening Wisdom" Triangle is an image that identifies the three necessary elements for listening development: Attitudes, Skills, and Knowledge. You can remember it easily with the acronym A-S-K.[3]

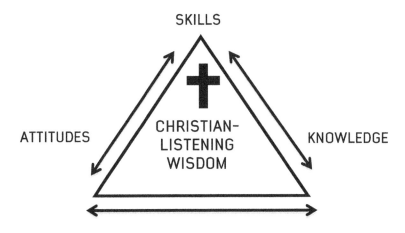

Attitudes inspire all behaviors. Christ-like attitudes inspire Christ-like behaviors. If you establish and practice positive attitudes when you listen, your relationships will thrive.

Skills consist of many listening behaviors and techniques necessary for you to succeed as an effective listener.

Knowledge expands your insight and understanding of specific facts that provide meaningful substance to the "who, what, why, where, and how" as you listen.

Continuously practicing all three elements is necessary in order to develop Christian-Listening Wisdom.

What Is Listening?

Having an understandable and effective definition of listening proves important in *BE QUICK TO LISTEN.* Listening is a natural and learned human behavior with five sequential steps: Sensing, Interpreting, Evaluating, Responding Appropriately to messages, and Remembering. This is known as SIER*.

Each of the parts of the definition combines to form a complete process of listening. Known as the SIER* process, it consists of four stages:[4]

- **SENSING** what God wants you to hear means that you use all your senses: sound, sight, smell, taste, and touch. It is not just hearing what someone is saying; you also must listen to verbal and non-verbal cues. In other words, sometimes you must "listen" to what you see. It's not just what others say; it's how they say it and how they show it. All other stages of listening will be affected favorably when sensing is complete and accurate. Once you use all your senses to take in the message, then you move on to the next stage.

- **INTERPRETING** is understanding or comprehending the message. What is this person saying? There are several skills you can use to interpret the message, including asking questions, encouraging the person to keep speaking, and paraphrasing (repeating back) and summarizing the message. The listener's task is to make sure his or her listening interpretation and understanding matches that of the sender. Once you are in alignment and fully understand, you move on to the next stage.

Listening = SIER*

SENSE
- Use all of your senses to take in the message: hear it, see it, smell it, taste it, touch it.
- Recognize not only what people say, but how they say it and show it.

INTERPRET
- Withhold judgement until your understanding is complete.
- Encourage the speaker to keep speaking.
- Clarify your understanding of the message (ask questions, repeat back in your own words, summarize and check for agreement).

EVALUATE
- Test the message against the evidence available.
- Probe with follow-up questions to deepen understanding.
- Identify if the message is a fact, an opinion, or a prediction.
- Take time to discern, to be confident that you have intentionally evaluated.
- Decide your response.

RESPOND
- Recognize that how you respond is not only what you say, but how you say it and show it.
- Before responding, ask yourself: "Will my response add value?" (If the answer is no, adjust what you say or show.)
- Take care to respond rather than react.
- Share your response with conscious intent.

M E M O R Y

If you choose to bring information into long term memory, consciously move it through each stage in the process.

©2012, Dr. Rick Bommelje   **LISTENING AID #1A**

- **EVALUATING** is making a judgment through the filter of God's Word about the message you have interpreted. Only after you have assured yourself that you have been sensing and interpreting accurately can you then move to evaluating. You have earned the right to discern the message. When *evaluating,* judgments are made. Basically, listeners will like or dislike, agree or disagree with, accept or reject speakers' messages. Is the sender credible? Is this a fact or an opinion? What is the evidence? How recent is it? Once you have faithfully considered these factors and have evaluated the message accurately, you move on to the next stage.

- **RESPONDING APPROPRIATELY** marks the final stage and includes what you say verbally or what you show nonverbally. Responding involves being appropriately intentional, thoughtful, alert, and controlled. This is much different from reacting, which is about being emotional, instinctive, impulsive, and uncontrolled. Pastor Neiner also emphasizes the importance of responding appropriately in his definition of Christian-Listening.

These four stages are connected together by memory or remembering. This is the asterisk. By continually moving through each stage in the process, you deposit what you want in your long-term memory bank.

The hourglass in the following graphic represents how you spend your time – it represents your life. The sand in the top is the future; the sand in the bottom is the past. The grains of sand flowing through the tube represent the present moment, otherwise known as the 'now.' SIER*ing occurs in the moment.

Time Opportunities to Apply SIER*

SIER* can be applied to your interactions in various ways.

← In the FUTURE:

Use SIER* to plan and develop your approach to important interactions.

← In the PRESENT:

Use SIER* to apply and deliver effective listening skills to be more effective in the moment.

← In the PAST:

Use SIER* to debrief your effectiveness and to diagnose communication problems.

Adapted from *Listening Leaders* by
Dr. Lyman K. Steil & Dr. Richard K. Bommelje

©2012, Dr. Rick Bommelje   **LISTENING AID #1B**

- **STORING*** is remembering what you have been "Sensing, Interpreting, and Evaluating" *if* you believe it is worth remembering. You deposit what you don't want to forget into your long-term memory bank so you can retrieve it at a later time.

Here are three tips that help ensure you are responding appropriately before you speak or show your nonverbal communication:

1. Use the Golden Pause (silence with a purpose) before you speak or show your nonverbal communication. It is the space between a stimulus and a response and enables you to choose how you would like to respond.

2. Ask yourself the question: "Will what I am about to say or show add value?"

3. Ask yourself the question: "Will what I am about to say or show improve the silence?"

When you learn and apply the listening definition in each relationship and directly connect it to your faith in God, Christian-Listening can transform your life. Without being equipped with listening knowledge and being mindful of the purpose of Christian-Listening, communication breakdowns occur, and the costs add up quickly.

LIFE APPLICATION

Carrie was seated at the conference room table. Glancing up at the wall clock and alternately at her watch, she wondered why no one else had joined her yet. As the meeting was set to begin in only five minutes, she mumbled to herself, "Maybe I'll be the only one here." Part of her wished that were true.

At first, she hesitated to get involved at her new church. Although she had been extensively involved in her hometown church, the company she worked for decided to move its headquarters, and now here she was, in a new town and a new church.

The meeting notice in the bulletin the previous Sunday had jumped out at her. A task force was being formed to put together a plan for the church to support the local homeless shelter. Since she had helped countless homeless persons at her previous church, she decided to attend to learn more about the ministry.

Stan walked in, abruptly ending Carrie's thoughts. "Where is everybody?" she asked. Stan smiled. "Hi, Carrie, nice to see you here," he replied. "Isn't anyone else coming?" Carrie shot back, continuing her interrogation. Stan politely responded that the meeting was not scheduled to start until 7:15 p.m.

No," Carrie answered. "The bulletin's calendar says 7 p.m."

"Yes, but Pastor Andy announced the time change at church on Sunday."

"Oh," Carrie responded. "I didn't know that." Carrie suddenly remembered that as soon as the congregation had begun singing the closing hymn last Sunday, she had started digging in her purse for her car keys. Spotting them, her eyes then glanced at her cell phone, and she saw the text message from her boss. She started answering it immediately as the pastor's voice became background noise.

By 7:20 p.m., Carrie realized that only a few empty seats were left at the table. She also realized that she didn't know anyone in the room except Stan. This situation was a far cry from the meetings she had attended at her previous church; Carrie knew just about everyone there and was usually the one facilitating. "Can we get started?" she blurted out.

Carrie had grown anxious. She was accustomed to having meetings start on time. Others in the room began introducing themselves to Carrie. She was still upset over the delay in the meeting's start time and had trouble remembering their names.

Stan opened the meeting with a devotion centered on Mark 9:41, *"I tell you the truth; anyone who gives you a cup of water in my name because you belong to Christ will certainly not lose his reward."* While Stan was talking about the verse, Carrie began looking around the room intently. She concentrated on trying to recall everyone's name; Stan's voice was merely a blur in her mind as she continued to mentally fidget.

Stan introduced the meeting agenda. The first item on the list was defining the task force goals; the second item was discussing the proposed timeline for completing their task.

It was estimated that their work would take about six months before their ideas could be presented to the church leaders. Looking straight at Stan, Carrie interrupted him in mid-sentence. "At my previous church," she contended, "we only took four months to do the same thing you're trying to do!"

Interrupting the flow of the meeting to respond to Carrie, he said, "All in all, it will only take four months; however, we had to consider the seasons of Advent and Lent. When they happen, we typically don't meet." Carrie rolled her eyes.

Stan worked his way through the agenda slowly. At almost every turn, Carrie interrupted and related in detail what she would do if she were chosen to lead this initiative. Stan and most of the people around the table were growing tired of her constant interruptions. During the meeting, she referred to the person sitting across from her as Megan; her name was Molly.

Then it happened. A cell phone rang. Almost instinctively, eyes turned to Carrie, who was digging in her seemingly bottomless purse to retrieve her ringing phone. Instead of switching off the phone, Carrie answered the call and began carrying on a conversation—during the meeting!

Molly had seen enough. As soon as Carrie ended the conversation and put her phone on the table, Molly said, "Carrie, everyone else here has turned off their phones to give Stan our full attention. I'm asking you to do the same."

Carrie reached for her phone and switched it off. Before she could say anything else, Molly added, "We're glad to have you here, Carrie; however, we adhere to some basic guidelines when we meet. One of them is to allow the speaker to finish before interrupting him."

By this time, Carrie was feeling humiliated. Even though Molly had spoken to her gently and kindly, she was embarrassed by Molly's remarks. As she looked around the table, she noticed others smiling at Molly, glad she had been brave enough to speak her mind.

As the meeting's end drew near, Stan asked everyone willing to serve on the task force to raise his or her hand. Carrie's hand shot up like a rocket being launched. Waving her arm wildly, she exclaimed, "I'll help. I have a passion in my heart for the homeless. My favorite verse—I don't know if you're familiar with it—is Mark 9:41, "*I tell you the truth, anyone who gives you a cup of water in my name because you belong to Christ will certainly not lose his reward.*"

Everyone stared at her in disbelief. As Carrie wondered why they were all gazing at her, seconds went by, but it seemed like hours. Stan was the first to break the silence. "Yes, we're all familiar with that verse. In fact, the meeting's opening devotion centered on that scripture."

Carrie was silent. She heard the words of the closing prayer and quickly left the conference room without talking to anyone. What was everyone else in the room thinking? If

Carrie only knew . . . well, she might have realized the cost of her poor listening: most of them weren't looking forward to serving with her.

LISTENING LIFE APPLICATION DEBRIEF

Carrie violated several of the fundamentals of Building Block #1, Build a Solid Foundation. Let's analyze her situation.

1. Carrie was not aware of the "Christian-Listening Wisdom" Triangle.

2. She did not practice the listening definition: *Listening is a natural and learned human behavior of <u>Sensing</u>, <u>Interpreting</u>, <u>Evaluating</u>, <u>Responding Appropriately</u>, and <u>Storing*</u> messages.*

3. Carrie had not been "Sensing" the pastor's message about the time change of the meeting as the Sunday service concluded since she was texting a response to her boss.

4. She was not "Sensing" the opening scripture verse in the meeting.

5. Carrie was not fully "Interpreting" the messages but jumped straight to "Evaluating" by mentally criticizing the way the meeting was being led.

6. She did not remember, or "store," the names of the committee members, incorrectly referring to Molly as Megan.

7. Carrie did not "Respond appropriately" throughout the meeting.

For her first meeting, Carrie created several costs through her listening behavior. She lost respect and credibility and isolated herself from the other members.

CALL FOR ACTION: BUILDING BLOCK #1

✧ Deeply listen to God and build your life on His words.

✧ Memorize the following verses:

   ○ *Therefore, everyone who hears these words of Mine and puts them into practice is like a wise man who built his house on the rock.* Matthew 7:24

   ○ *So, then faith cometh by hearing; hearing by the Word of God.* Romans 10:17

   ○ *I will hear what the Lord will speak, for He will speak peace unto His people and to His saints. But let them not turn again to folly.* Psalm 85:8

- ✧ Re-read the story of Jesus Calling the Disciples in Matthew 4:18-20 and Luke 5:1-6.

- ✧ From Pastor Neiner's interview, identify at least one or two of his application points and put them into practice.

- ✧ Learn and apply the "Christian-Listening Wisdom" Triangle in all your relationships, and focus on the combination of your Attitudes, Skills, and Knowledge.

- ✧ Learn and apply the listening definition consistently.

- ✧ Monitor your listening results in all your relationships.

CLOSING PRAYER

Lord, teach me to listen to You and Your Word throughout the day. Help me to go from being an observer to a participant, to serve those around me and love them by my listening. Help me to live a life that is pleasing to You. Amen.

DEVELOP HEALTHY HABITS

2

"Your attitude should be the same as that of Christ Jesus." **Philippians 2:5 (NIV)**

The second Building Block in the series of six is Develop Healthy Habits. Attitude, which is connected directly to "habit," is actually a filter in your subconscious mind that processes all incoming information. To develop a certain attitude requires a consistent and constant thought process, repeated over and over again, until it moves from the conscious mind to the subconscious.

To establish a new attitude, an eventual habit requires an intentional discipline of thinking a new thought. Repetition is the key to allowing a behavior to become second nature. For example, a new thought might be, "Today, I am exactly who God says I am. I am no more than that, and very importantly, I am never, ever any less. God desires for me to listen to Him. Each day, I struggle and strive to listen the way God has called me to listen: with the attitude of Christ." This new attitude is developed and sustained by new habits. One habit might be disciplining yourself to spend time reading God's Word daily.

Christian-Listening enhances your life—at home, work, and school, and in your faith community. By consistently exercising discipline, your faith life will be enriched, and your heart and mind will be transformed.

Your attitude toward life circumstances and relationships

should be like the Lord's as defined by scripture: positive, encouraging, loving, humble, teachable, cooperative, self-sacrificing, and considerate. To do this willingly, consistently, and subconsciously, you need a new attitude. This approach will usher in strong, positive habits and incline your ears to listen to the Word of God.

BIBLE APPLICATION:
WHO IS THE GREATEST?

Jesus' disciples want to be in control. While on the road to Capernaum one day, they begin arguing about who is the greatest. In the life of Jewish groups at that time, questions of rank and status were normal. However, such questions have no place in Jesus' value system.

In Mark 9:33-37, you can visualize the disciples' ongoing debate over who is the greatest:

"Let one of us sit at your right, the other at your left in Your Glory."

"They came to Capernaum. When He was in the house, He asked them, "What were you arguing about on the road?" But they kept quiet because on the way they had argued about who was the greatest.

"Sitting down, Jesus called the Twelve and said, "Anyone who wants to be first must be the very last, and the servant of all."

"He took a little child whom He placed among them. Taking the child in His arms, He said to them, "Whoever welcomes one of these little children in my name welcomes me; and whoever welcomes me does not welcome me but the one who sent me."

The debate continues in the next chapter in Mark 10:35-41:

"Then James and John, the sons of Zebedee, came to Him. "Teacher," they said, "we want You to do for us whatever we ask." "What do you want Me to do for you?" He asked.

"They replied, "Let one of us sit at your right and the other at your left in Your Glory."

"You don't know what you are asking," Jesus said. "Can you drink the cup I drink or be baptized with the baptism I am baptized with?"

"We can," they answered. Jesus said to them, "You will drink the cup I drink and be baptized with the baptism I am baptized with, but to sit at" my right or left is not for Me to grant. These places belong to those for whom they have been prepared."

"When the ten heard about this, they became indignant with James and John. Jesus called them together and said, "You know that those who are regarded as rulers of the Gentiles lord it over them, and their high officials exercise authority over them.

Not so with you. Instead, whoever wants to become great among you must be your servant, and whoever wants to be first must be slave of all. The Son of Man did not come to be served, but to serve, and to give His life as a ransom for many."

The disciples' debate of "who is the greatest" flows directly out of their sinful nature. This same old, sinful nature is also yours; it's how you came out of the womb. It's reinforced in each of us over and over again by our view that life is a struggle to achieve our own greatness, however it's defined.

To do great things for and with God and with a new attitude requires a foundation of Christian-Listening. Herein lies the result: a strong, positive habit that overcomes your need to be in control, to lord it over others, and to be the greatest. Instead you will live in the strength, peace, and confidence of who you are in Christ.

PASTOR'S LISTENING PERSPECTIVE

Rev. Dr. Bob Henry is a Quaker pastor at Indianapolis First Friends in Indianapolis, Indiana. For members of the Quaker faith, listening to God and discerning His voice is fostered by a series of personal and communal disciplines—attainable only through repeated habits.

I would define Christian-Listening as "expectant waiting on what the Lord is saying to us through our lives, other people, and the scriptures." It often takes putting ourselves in a place where we can be silent, center ourselves, remove distractions, and focus on what God is trying to say. As Quakers, we are always trying to connect with the Inner Light of Christ—it is listening to that Light within us that helps guide us to the Spirit's leading. Listening, truly listening, to other people requires one to set aside preconceptions, challenge unspoken assumptions, and confront inward biases. In other words, listening to others is built first upon listening to oneself.

Sometimes we are too distracted, and listening on our own is impossible, so we need others to help listen with us; Quakers call this a "clearness committee," where a community of people gather to help one listen to what God is saying to them and discern together on what they are hearing. That means sometimes listening is a personal act and sometimes it is a communal discipline.

The "Listening" Bible verses that stand out to me are Psalm 46:10: "Be still and know that I am God." Listening begins with being in a posture to hear. Psalm 5:3: "In the morning, Lord, you hear my voice; in the morning, I lay my requests before you and wait expectantly.

Speaking comes naturally but listening is a discipline. "What you have said in the dark will be heard in the daylight, and what you have whispered in the ear in the inner rooms will be proclaimed from the roofs." Luke 12:3. The inner Light of Christ speaks to us, and what we hear is God speaking to our inner lives and is what we are to proclaim and live in our daily lives.

I believe the discipline of listening must begin with finding a way to "center down" and put one's self in a position to listen. Silent meditation on what God is speaking to us is key. To slow our lives, our distractions, our technology, anything that gets in the way, is key to us being able to listen.

That means the Christian-listener will need to commit to seeking that place in their soul and in their daily lives.

I would again suggest "clearness committees" (a group of women and men appointed to help a person listen and find clarity around a leading). The discipline may start with us but may be shared with others. We need our community of faith to speak into our lives in this way—and this, too, is a discipline.

The outcome of Christian-Listening is "peace of mind and soul," or clearness. We have so much vying for our attention in this world. Clarity is so important to feeling empowered to respond to what God and our neighbor are saying.

Also, when we listen, we become more aware of what we are thinking, what God is saying, and what the world needs. It helps build community and friendship and ultimately TRUST. But I sense in our day and age the biggest outcome would be peace in our daily situations.

Measuring Christian-Listening seems to be a daunting task, but I sense that there are personal goals and communal commitments that may be measured if studied. Disciplining one's self by keeping a personal journal or conversation log with others may help in seeing outcomes over time and what are the best practices for hearing each other and God.

Since listening is key to Quaker worship and life; each time we meet for worship, we take time to sit silently, center down, and begin with a time of expectant waiting and listening for the Spirit. I also teach the importance of waiting to answer or respond to others by taking a pause before sharing your thoughts. This pause shows you are committed to listening to your neighbor and to what God may be saying. I also encourage people to find freedom from technology, slow the pace of life, and take time to find a space to meditate and listen to God daily. Silence, solitude, and meditation are key disciplines for Quakers, and I practice and emphasize them in community weekly.

One of the listening breakdowns that I experienced was a time when I stopped listening to my own inner life and thought I had control. I stopped relying on the Spirit's leading and prompting and took things into my own hands. I found out the hard way through burnout, a lack of self-awareness, and personal pain that my life needs disciplined space to listen, be silent, and meditate—to be better prepared and able to effectively minister to those around me.

In today's world, I believe there are three significant distractions that prevent Christians from effectively listening:

1. *Technology – Social media, email, etc., give us more information but little space to listen. They fill our lives with extra stuff but not always the important items that come from listening.*
2. *Daily Busyness – We are busier today than ever. Our fast-paced life needs slowing—and that means church and spiritual practices as well.*
3. *Consumerism – We are fixated on the need to have more. We can't find time to listen if we are always wanting more and seeking more. Listening is a humbling act that diverts the attention from us and makes us vulnerable to the possibilities of what God and others are saying.*

The most important behavior that the Christian-listener can develop as a daily practice is awareness. Being self-differentiated is key to developing listening as a daily practice. Knowing who you are and what your traits, behaviors, and feelings indicate about yourself and your ability to listen have been the most important aspect of Christian-Listening and impacting the Kingdom of God. Knowing one's self and being confident in who God made you are the most important aspect.

Being a Quaker minister, I have worked diligently on learning to listen and help model listening, but I will be honest, listening does not come easy. Too often my mind is filled with thoughts, ideas, teachings, and ways to help or fix problems, but most of the time I would be a better minister if I listened more and spoke less. I think part of that is my extroverted-ness, yet I am learning to embrace my shadow side and allow more space for listening and preparing to listen in my life.

LISTENING KNOWLEDGE

In order to BE QUICK TO LISTEN, it is important to establish healthy habits. The first step is to assess your current listening habits. Respond to the following questions on this "Listening Habits Profile©" to gain insight into what you're doing or not doing when you listen.

10 Healthy Listening Habits Profile[5]

One way to become a better listening leader is to analyze the factors that distinguish the effective listeners from the ineffective ones. Respond to the following questions to measure how often you engage in each habit. Check yourself carefully on each one.

HABIT	FREQUENCY					SCORE
	Almost Always	Usually	Sometime	Seldom	Almost Never	
1. How often do you find the speaker's subject uninteresting?	☐	☐	☐	☐	☐	————
2. How often do you criticize the speaker's speaking skills (in your own mind)?	☐	☐	☐	☐	☐	————
3. How often do you get over-stimulated by something the speaker says?	☐	☐	☐	☐	☐	————
4. How often do you listen only for facts?	☐	☐	☐	☐	☐	————
5. How often do you find yourself not taking notes?	☐	☐	☐	☐	☐	————
6. How often do you fake attention to the speaker?	☐	☐	☐	☐	☐	————
7. How often do you tolerate distractions?	☐	☐	☐	☐	☐	————
8. How often do you avoid listening to difficult material?	☐	☐	☐	☐	☐	————
9. How often do you find your emotions working against what you're listening to?	☐	☐	☐	☐	☐	————
10. How often does your mind wander when you listen?	☐	☐	☐	☐	☐	————

Listening Habits Profile Scoring Key

- ☐ For every "ALMOST ALWAYS" checked, add 2 points.
- ☐ For every "USUALLY" checked, add 4 points.
- ☐ For every "SOMETIMES" checked, add 6 points.
- ☐ For every "SELDOM" checked, add 8 points.
- ☐ For every "ALMOST NEVER" checked, add 10 points.

Add up all 10 items for a Total Score:

What Your Score Means

Results from the thousands of leaders who have completed this Listening Habits Profile produced an average score of 62. As you evaluate your answers and your score, consider the impact of your habits. If you scored:

100 - 90   Congratulations! You are a GREAT listener who understands and utilizes the power of listening. Your listening habits serve you well and deserve conscious repetition. Your greatest opportunity is to develop the discipline to consistently practice the "10 Healthy Listening Habits" and then share that knowledge with others.

88 - 80   VERY GOOD. You are significantly above average in practicing effective listening habits. As you continue to practice this

discipline, you will enhance your life and the lives of those around you. Additional focus on your listening limitations will bring unexpected blessings and unanticipated joy. Developing healthy listening habits always begins with daily discipline.

78 - 70   Consider yourself a GOOD listener. Your habits serve you better than many. However, you have specific negative listening habits that negate your positive and productive habits. With special attention, willingness, self-sacrifice, and practice, you can quickly make progress and increase your score. Developing healthy listening habits begins with making a commitment, building on your strengths, and tapping into the power of God within you.

68- 60   Get ready to work because you fall into the land of FAIR. As a listener, the bad news/good news should be clear. The bad news is the simple fact that fair listening relegates you to the average rank of listeners. The good news is you have identified specific opportunities for development.

Moreover, your conscious discipline will provide significant returns. FAIR listeners possess the benefit, potential, and opportunity of miraculous transformation. By putting your energies into building new listening habits, you will be blessed immensely. Developing healthy listening habits begins with making a promise to improve.

Below 60   POOR. The further you score below the average of 62, the greater your challenge. Your task is formidable, yet clear and simple.

First, identify your areas of listening strengths, and solidify and hone your positive habits. Second, focus on the critical areas where you scored lowest. Third, recognize the negative impact, and establish a specific game plan to move the negative behaviors and habits to neutral and then to positive. Finally, track the results and rewards of changing the negative habits to positive habits. Developing healthy listening habits begins by facing the facts and then resolving to remedy the negatives.

Now that you have your score, you're ready for the following guidance:

10 Healthy Listening Habits

1. **FIND SOMETHING OF INTEREST:** Effective listeners are searchers and seekers. They are continuous learners who cultivate a listening habit out of compassion, curiosity, and caring.

2. **JUDGE CONTENT, NOT DELIVERY**: Effective listeners focus primarily on the content of a message and consider the delivery as secondary. They focus on what is being said, not the person saying it.

3. **WITHHOLD JUDGMENT**: Effective listeners don't jump to conclusions while the speaker delivers the message. They avoid making judgments until they fully understand the message.

4. **LISTEN FOR THE MAIN POINT**: Effective listeners identify the speaker's purpose and listen for main themes, not just facts. When people communicate, they sometimes include facts that are not relevant to their message. Trying to remember extraneous information can clutter your mind and take the focus off the speaker's main point.

5. **TAKE NOTES—WRITTEN AND/OR MENTAL**: Effective listeners take meaningful notes and adjust to the speaker. They also review their notes later. This habit helps to reinforce what the speaker is saying. Notes also become invaluable when it's your turn to speak.

6. **PAY CAREFUL ATTENTION**: Effective listeners give genuine, sincere, and heightened attention to every situation in which they choose to engage. Body movement, hand

motions, and facial expressions can often enhance the speaker's message. If your eyes are fixed on the speaker, you will not miss any of these gestures.

7. **RESIST DISTRACTIONS**: Effective listeners proactively identify distractions and take action to minimize or eliminate them. These are both external distractions (i.e., noise) and internal distractions (i.e., negative thoughts).

8. **EXERCISE YOUR MIND**: Effective listeners seek out the challenging and difficult. They consciously and constantly exercise their mind's listening muscle. They listen even when they don't feel like listening.

9. **CHECK YOUR EMOTIONS**: Effective listeners have established the habit of leading their emotions rather than have their emotions lead them. They know how to keep both their negative and positive emotions in check. They disregard any preconceived notions or ideas they have about the speaker or the subject of the message. They listen as though every conversation starts off with a clean slate.

10. **UTILIZE THE GAP BETWEEN SPEECH SPEED and LISTENING SPEED**: The average person can listen and comprehend up to 400 words per minute. This is nearly three to four times faster than the average person speaks. Effective listeners use this gap to their

advantage. They use the extra processing time to ensure they have comprehended the message.

Effective listeners consciously shape their listening habits. They focus on the "10 Healthy Listening Habits" and resolve to excel in each one of them.

LIFE APPLICATION

John was not looking forward to attending this Saturday's workshop. He wanted to stay home, watch football, and put his feet up in his comfy leather recliner.

After all, he'd had a rough workweek. Meetings after meetings intruded on each day, from the time he arrived until the time he left. He considered them all a waste of time; nothing much ever got accomplished. That lack of accomplishment left him frustrated and moody.

He had only been half-joking when he told his wife, Anna, that he was going to start his own Facebook page. He really wasn't joking though. John was reacting to Anna's obsession with social networking. He wondered what held her interest for hours on end, night after night. John knew Anna enjoyed keeping up with her siblings who were scattered across the globe. But, he didn't understand the deep and powerful attraction.

"I'm going to sign you up for a workshop at our local library. It's all about social networking and more specifically, Facebook. That way you can learn about it, too. You might be able to connect with those Army buddies of yours from your time in Vietnam, who you talk about so often," Anna quipped quite unexpectedly one morning.

John was caught off guard. "What?" he asked. "Don't do that. I'm really not interested in attending a workshop, especially on a Saturday. No way. Besides, I could be doing other things with my valuable time."

Unprepared for John's reaction, Anna thought he'd have a more positive response to her idea. After all, she was just trying to help him reconnect with the men he served with in the Army. He often talked about how much these buddies meant to him. "If nothing else, do it for me," she said.

So, John, armed with a bad mood and grumpy attitude, pulled into the library's parking lot Saturday morning. He hastily stepped out of the car and bolted through the building's glass doors. "Where's that Facebook thing?" he gruffly asked the librarian sitting at the Reference Desk.

"Down the hall, first door on the left," she said politely. In a half-whispering tone, she added, "Room 1B. I'm sure you'll enjoy the speaker. He's a great resource for all of us trying to make sense of this social networking stuff." With no attempt at friendliness, John ignored her assistance. He turned around, mumbled something under his breath, and stomped defiantly down the hallway to Room 1B.

Upon entering the room, his eyes darted nervously left and right. With only two empty seats, the room was much more crowded than he anticipated. John slouched down into a chair. "Okay, I'm here. I hope Anna's satisfied. What a waste of time!" he mumbled.

Angie, seated next to John, was doodling in her notepad and dared not look his way. The only words she could make out from John's hushed tirade were "Anna" and "waste of time." She wasn't looking forward to the next 90 minutes seated next to a guy who resented being there. "If he disturbs me, I'll just have to say something to him," she thought.

The workshop facilitator entered the room with a hearty "hello!" to everyone. All the voices in the room replied to him, it seemed, with the exception of John's. By this time, he'd resolved not to participate; he'd just pass the time thinking about the football game he was missing, a strategy that didn't make him feel any better about being there.

John noticed that the instructor was wearing two sweaters, corduroy pants and a woolen scarf hugging his neck tightly. "Probably some sort of computer geek," he thought. While the instructor talked, he couldn't keep his eyes off the outer sweater, which was way too big for the small-framed man. Maybe it belonged to his grandfather or uncle. In addition, it's flaming red hue reminded him of the Santa suit he donned for his boys each Christmas. As John sized up the instructor's wardrobe, he heard him say, "Buddies."

"What'd he say?" John asked himself as he shifted from a slouching to a sitting position to hear the instructor better. It was the same thing Anna had told him: social networking would be a great way to try to reunite with his Army buddies. Now John began to listen.

After this, he never noticed the instructor's clothing again. He was listening so intently that the man's sweater, about three sizes too big for him, no longer mattered. Connectedness! That was what the instructor was talking about. He was talking about how social networking can connect you to people all around the world, rekindling relationships, and even finding lost relatives and high school sweethearts.

As the instructor continued, John realized he was saying things that he wanted to remember to do later at home. Politely, he asked Angie if he could have a piece of paper from her notepad. She willingly obliged because the grumpy man next to her had transformed into a smiling, pleasant workshop partner.

John raised his hand, asking the instructor to repeat the link he had to type in. He wanted to be sure he got it correctly, so he checked his notes carefully as the facilitator repeated himself. The more John listened, the more excited he became at the prospect of reuniting with the guys he spent so much time with overseas. The football game crossed his mind a few times, but he basically had forgotten all about it.

As the 90 minutes drew to a close, John raised his hand. "Yes? I could tell you wanted to raise your hand several times to ask a question. Thanks for waiting until the end and not interrupting me," the facilitator said, acknowledging him.

John asked him if he personally knew of anyone who had

connected with long-lost friends using social networking. He mentioned that he was anxious to try and find his Army buddies.

The facilitator relayed one story about two girls he knew who were separated at birth and put into different foster homes. They found each other through a social networking site, *Reunited,* and are now living in the same town. Dozens of hands shot up in the air. Each person had his or her own tale about connecting with someone with whom they'd lost contact.

The atmosphere in the classroom had changed. There was laughter and even some tears at the mention of mothers and fathers who'd found the children they had given up for adoption. Although John was interested, he wanted to get home and go online to set up his profile.

He hurried to his car and started driving home with only one stop along the way. As he opened the front door, Anna was standing nearby. Considering the way he had left the house, she feared what he'd be like when stepped into the room. She quickly found out when he pulled a bouquet of flowers from behind his back and presented her with them. "Thanks, Anna, for signing me up for that workshop. I really enjoyed listening to the instructor and learned a lot." Anna accepted the flowers, smiling to herself. She was going to say that she had been right all along, but he probably wouldn't have heard her.

LISTENING LIFE APPLICATION DEBRIEF

John was unenthusiastic and reluctantly compliant as he entered the Facebook workshop. However, after he was able to finally understand the benefit of what social networking could do for him and the prospect of re-connecting with his Army buddies, he shifted from an observer to a fully engaged participant. Following are the listening habits John practiced:

1. **Find something of interest** – After the instructor said the word "buddies," he immediately realized the value of the workshop. His buddies had met yearly since the end of the Vietnam War, and he wanted to be included.

2. **Content first, delivery second** – John initially was mentally criticizing what the instructor was wearing. As he became more interested in the workshop, the instructor's attire became less significant to him.

3. **Take notes** – He asked Angie for a sheet of paper to take notes.

4. **Pay careful attention** - When he understood the potential of what Facebook could do for him and his buddies, he was totally engaged.

5. **Resist distractions** – John shifted away from thinking about the football game and focused on the workshop.

CALL FOR ACTION: BUILDING BLOCK #2

✧ Through the spiritual discipline of listening, develop the attitude to do great things for and with God through your listening.

✧ Memorize the following verses:

- *Your attitude should be the same as that of Christ Jesus.* Philippians 2:5

- *Be still and know that I am God.* Psalm 46:10

- *In the morning, Lord, you hear my voice; in the morning, I lay my requests before you and wait expectantly.* Psalm 5:3

- *What you have said in the dark will be heard in the daylight, and what you have whispered in the ear in the inner rooms will be proclaimed from the roofs.* Luke 12:3

✧ Re-read the story of Jesus calling the Disciples in Mark 9:33-37 and Mark 10:35-41.

✧ From Dr. Henry's interview, identify at least one or two of his application points and put them into practice.

✧ Learn and apply the "10 Healthy Listening Habits," especially those which you scored the lowest on in the "10 Healthy Listening Habits Profile."

✧ Monitor your attitude and your listening habits in all your relationships.

CLOSING PRAYER

Father, I am who You say I am—no more, but never, ever any less. Please help me create the habit of having a Christ-like attitude as I listen to those whom You put in my path. Listening to You cultivates a new attitude. I desire to do great things for and with You. Help me to listen for Your response, to not get so busy, distracted, and self-centered that I can't hear You. These things I pray, in Jesus' name. Amen.

TAKE 100% RESPONSIBILITY

3

"Then Jesus said, 'Whoever has ears to hear, let them hear.'" Mark 4:9 (NIV)

To BE QUICK TO LISTEN, it's necessary to be personally responsible for your listening. The third building block is to Take 100% Responsibility when you listen. In the central scripture verse for the third Building Block, Jesus is calling for people to pay careful attention. It's another way of Him saying, "It's time to listen up!"

Jesus spoke in parables because he sought to gain His listeners' attention, using familiar images, everyday objects, or human emotions to inform them. They loved stories, and the parables represented characters and happenings with which they could easily relate. But unless they were willing to come to Jesus with a commitment to take 100% responsibility for understanding the meaning of His preaching, His words would only amount to empty stories. They needed more than ears; they needed ears to hear.

Just exactly *who* is "whoever who has ears"? The simple answer is "all people who are being given the Words of God." Like the parables' original audience, you must use your eyes to see and ears to hear in order to tune in to His words.

BIBLE APPLICATION:
THE PARABLE OF THE SOWER

"Whoever has ears to hear, let him hear."

Again, Jesus began to teach by the lake. The crowd that gathered around Him was so large that He got into a boat and sat in it out on the lake, while all the people were along the shore at the water's edge. He taught them many things by parables, and in His teaching said: "Listen! A farmer went out to sow his seed. As he was scattering the seed, some fell along the path, and the birds came and ate it up. Some fell on rocky places, where it did not have much soil. It sprang up quickly, because the soil was shallow. But when the sun came up, the plants were scorched, and they withered because they had no root. Other seed fell among thorns, which grew up and choked the plants, so that they did not bear grain. Still other seed fell on good soil. It came up, grew and produced a crop, some multiplying thirty, some sixty, some a hundred times." Then Jesus said, "Whoever has ears to hear, let them hear."

When He was alone, the Twelve and the others around Him asked Him about the parables. He told them, "The secret of the Kingdom of God has been given to you. But to those on the outside everything is said in parables so that,

"'They may be ever seeing but never perceiving, and ever hearing but never understanding; otherwise they might turn and be forgiven!'"

Then Jesus said to them, "Don't you understand this parable? How then will you understand any parable? The farmer sows the Word. Some people are like seed along the path, where the Word is sown. As soon as they hear it, Satan comes and takes away the Word that was sown in them. Others, like seed sown on rocky places, hear the Word and at once receive it with joy. But since they have no root, they last only a short time.

When trouble or persecution comes because of the Word, they quickly fall away. Still others, like seed sown among thorns, hear the Word; but the worries of this life, the deceitfulness of wealth, and the desires for other things come in and choke the Word, making it unfruitful. Others, like seed sown on good soil, hear the Word, accept it, and produce a crop—some thirty, some sixty, some a hundred times what was sown." Mark 4:1-20

Jesus teaches in parables to conceal the secret of the Kingdom from "those outside." Their hidden meanings are concealed from those who doubt Him. Seeking God's truth takes energy and focus. It takes a conscious commitment and a steadfast willingness to be challenged and changed. There is a difference between having ears and having "ears to hear." In the Parable of the Sower, Jesus is distinguishing between four types of hearers.[6]

1. **Hard Path Hearers** – Some people hear the truth, but like hardened paths of rocks and stones, they do not let it sink into their hearts. Soon Satan takes the truth away. (In the Bible, birds are sometimes a picture of satan.) If people do not receive and respond to the Word with "ears" of faith, their opportunity will be stolen by the evil one. They immediately forget the message. It goes in one ear and out the other.

2. **Rocky Place Hearers** – These people take great joy in hearing the message, but like seeds on rocky soil, it does not take root. When they face life's pressures or tough challenges, they quickly forget about God's Word. They quickly drop out when they realize that it requires hard work to be Christ-like. A true believer follows Jesus no matter what.

3. **Thorny Hearers** – They hear God's Word and begin to bear fruit. However, they quickly get bogged down in the worries of daily life, which consumes them. They get mired in the weeds and do not focus on what really matters most.

4. **Responsible and Responsive Hearers** – They move from being hearers of the Word to doers and use their God-given talents to bear fruit.

The Christian-listener personifies the fourth type of hearer and takes 100% responsibility to deeply listen to God's Word and apply its message; thus, this integrity in listening responsibility and responsiveness permeates listening situations with others.

PASTOR'S LISTENING PERSPECTIVE

Tim DeTellis is an author and speaker, encouraging others to live life to the fullest. An ordained Southern Baptist minister, he serves as president of New Missions based in Orlando, FL.

Christian-Listening is hearing what God wants for me because the confusing filter is my bias or my agenda. It's a daily surrender to God. I need to first align myself with what God wants in my life and what God would want in other people's lives. When I think about the discipline of a Christian-listener, I think about an alignment to Jesus being Lord of your life. So, the question I ask myself is, "Who am I listening to for guidance first?" I need to go to God first and seek wise counsel.

There is a pause I tend to make in a conversation, or even in a situation I may be in, where there's a sense of either confusion or stress. I always ask, "God, what is Your will?"

By asking the Lord, it brings me back to a prayer I pray daily, which is how Jesus taught His disciples to pray in The Lord's Prayer. A big foundation of that prayer is "Thy will be done on earth as it is in heaven." We have to go back to "What is the will of God in our lives?" So, in the middle of a circumstance, I need to go back to the question, "What is God's will in this circumstance?"

That's the question I'll ask myself frequently. I pray that I'll be prompted to yield to His Spirit to navigate—to know what the best decision may be, or even how to listen to that person to help calm the situation, or how to ask the next question to bring more clarity and to bring more peace. I've been praying The Lord's Prayer daily for two years. What I have found is that I have more trust now with God's orchestrations in my life than with my own strategy, and it's helped bring me a lot of peace. I may have a plan, but I have to understand that, within that plan, His purpose will be greater, and He'll navigate me through what may even be a distraction of my own agenda.

When I think about listening, a few Bible verses stand out in my mind:

Psalm 46:10. "Be still and know that I am God. I will be exalted among the nations. I will be exalted in all the earth." The "be still" portion of that is what really helped set the tone for me on listening.

Another is Luke 11:28. "Blessed rather are those who hear the Word of God and obey it." We're blessed when we hear, but we can't hear unless we listen and be still. That is a reward; that is a gift. I'm convinced that there is so much to be heard already from just the Word of God that's already been written.

I also like Proverbs 25:12. It says, "Like a gold ring or an ornament of gold is a wise reprover to a listening ear." If you're a listening person, you're going to reap the reward.

To me, being silent is the single most important behavior that a Christian-listener can develop as a daily practice. When we're silent, we then can tune in. One of my favorite places to go is in my backyard, which is surrounded by citrus and trees, and I love the sunrise in the morning. I'll be silent, and I can hear the noise of that environment, the beauty of the environment, the space and the nature. I overcome whatever noise I may already have in my heart and my mind. I feel the presence of God.

The outcome of Christian-Listening can be challenging because we tend to want to think about outcome as progress, success, or results, as if we're achieving something. In scripture, one of the teachings of Christ that really has spoken to me recently is the fruit of the Spirit: love, joy, peace, patience, kindness, goodness, faithfulness, gentleness, and self-control.

As we yield more to His Spirit in our lives, what is the outcome? How does that manifest itself in our daily living? As I am listening to God, I receive the result—the fruit of the Spirit—because when I'm more in tune to Him and His will, I can feel a greater love because it's what He wants for my life. I can also feel a greater peace because all the other confusing voices or stresses go away. There's a sense of gentleness toward others because I don't need to force them into something because I'm aiming for God's will. I have patience with people because I want them to find God's will for their life, and I want to be patient with myself to find God's will. You get a sense of faithfulness, joy, goodness, kindness, patience, and self-control. To me, that's really the way that I would measure the outcome of Christian-Listening in my life.

Christian-Listening has given me peace with God and others. Often, I can become confused when I seek other people's acceptance or even to have influence over other people for a goal or an agenda. In our organization, we are not motivated by growth. We're motivated by impact that is all about listening.

For example, I was in Haiti recently, and there was a baptism festival. The pastors of our churches who had gathered for the festival were clearly instructed months prior that this wasn't a competition in terms of which church could bring the most people to get baptized.

We can be motivated for results, and that's the metrics— for our own reward—to make sure you look good, feel good, feel successful. Rather, it is about listening to the lives of those they serve, so that the believers' baptisms have a real public profession of their faith and devotion to God because that's God's will. That's what's real in their life versus selling them on an idea. It helps us align ourselves to why we're here.

I go back to The Lord's Prayer. It is "Thy Kingdom come, Thy will be done." Our purpose is to be a part of His Kingdom, and there is only one CEO." One of my favorite verses is Colossians 3:23-24: "Do what you do unto the Lord, not unto man." So, we're working for God. It's His agenda, and it's His goal and mission.

LISTENING KNOWLEDGE

To BE QUICK TO LISTEN, Christian-listeners recognize that there are five purposes of communication: information, social, emotional, persuasive, and entertainment. Each purpose fulfills an important mission:

1. **Informative:** Deals with facts, details, and ideas.

2. **Social:** Includes the "small talk of life" such as the weather, news, sports, movies, and other everyday topics of conversation; also provides the bridge to emotional and persuasive communication.

3. **Emotional:** Deals with sharing feelings with others, either listening with empathy or expressing emotion.

4. **Persuasive:** Involves one person trying to influence another.

5. **Entertaining:** Includes listening and speaking to gain appreciation and pleasure.

It is important for Christian-listeners to take 100% responsibility to identify the other person's purpose for communicating so that they can fully understand his or her message and intent.

Five Purposes of Communication[7]

In the diagram above, the four purposes are divided into halves, which represent the specific roles you play in any communication: listener and speaker:

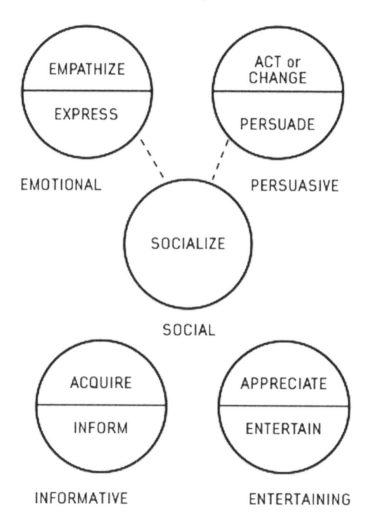

♦ If your intent is to *inform* as you speak, and the other person doesn't *acquire* your message as she listens, then the interaction has failed as informative communication.

- ✧ If your intent is to *express* emotion, and the other person doesn't *empathize* with your message, then the interaction has failed as emotional communication.

- ✧ If your intent is to *persuade*, and the other person doesn't *act or change* based on your message, then the interaction has failed as persuasive communication.

- ✧ If your intent is to *entertain*, and the other person doesn't *appreciate* your message, then the interaction has failed as entertaining communication.

- ✧ Also, with social communication, if either the speaker or the listener does not desire to *socialize* or build rapport, a breakdown will occur.

Social communication isn't shown as having two halves like the others because the roles of speaker and listener switch back and forth quickly. The intent of both parties is only to socialize. However, in the process, social communication can build relationships.

Social communication is known as the bridge-building purpose, which is why dotted lines extend from it to emotional and persuasive communication. Very rarely will people vent their feelings to you unless some kind of relationship has been established. Influencing others also proves very difficult without some previous relationship being built. That's why it's helpful to know something about the people with whom we interact.

Understanding the other person's purpose can help you understand his or her role in the communication. It also shows that both people need to play their part for the communication to be purposeful. When both people play their part well, a benefit can result. When one person in the communication doesn't play his or her part—doesn't care about the message or the other person's response—a cost ensues. Communication breakdowns generally occur when the speaker and listener stand at cross-purposes.

The illustration of the medieval castle on the next page provides another way to view the five purposes. Think of yourself and everyone around you as being like the castle. On any typical day, you encounter numerous acquaintances, strangers, and other "outsiders"—people with whom you don't have particularly strong relationships.

And in general, it's easy for you to get information or entertainment from these people. Out in the world, people's agendas can be hidden or out in the open; it doesn't matter, because you don't—and can't—have relationships with everyone.

*If you want to be invited inside the castle,
you must engage the guard.*

But consider the fraction of the population with whom you *do* have relationships. How do you get to know them? How do you decide whether or not you want to invite them inside your castle?

Social communication helps you decide whom you want to let in and whom you want to keep out. The "small talk" of life is what helps you get to know people. When you take the time to become familiar with people, you uncover shared values and build trust and rapport. In the process, you let your guard down, and when you do this, you are letting someone inside your castle. That means you are ready to have an emotional connection with them, or that you trust them enough to let them persuade you—or be persuaded by you. And those people become your family, friends, and partners.

You can't build a relationship after just one meeting, and you can't build *trusting* relationships when your communication is at cross-purposes. Social communication lets you get to know others—*and helps them get to know you*—in a way that is safe.

Over time, the guard comes down so you can enjoy stronger emotional bonds and greater influence. You become an "insider" in somebody else's castle, and they become one in yours.

The same is true about your relationship with God. You can't build a relationship after encountering Him one time a year—at Christmas? Easter? Until you let your guard down and acknowledge that you need a Savior in your life, the relationship remains estranged.

LIFE APPLICATION

Anne stood in the room's far corner while the other attendees congregated in small groups. They were so absorbed in laughter and conversation that Anne was sure she could swiftly navigate around them and slip through the doors across the room without being noticed.

She decided to move quickly and was about to take her first stride when a man stepped in front of her. Anne was startled by his sudden appearance and stopped dead in her tracks. He was holding a tray of appetizers that looked very inviting.

After hurriedly placing several of them on a plate, she headed toward the doors, slipped through to the other side, and let out a huge sigh of relief.

Having safely made her way outdoors, Anne tried to rationalize why she had responded to the notice in the Sunday church bulletin about the young adults' get-together. The gathering was at the home of one of her closest friends, Kristi. She didn't want to disappoint her, but she also dreaded going to social events. Now, she was beginning to wonder if it were worth it. Even though she stood on the patio beneath the starlit sky, it would only be a matter of time before she would have to face the inescapable. Someone was going to notice her, strike up a conversation, and expect her to listen and respond.

Out of the corner of Barry's eye, he saw a woman he thought he recognized standing by herself on the patio. He excused himself from his friends, navigated through the crowd, and slipped outside.

Anne could sense someone right behind her. She stood perfectly still, half expecting this uninvited patio intruder to walk away. That was not the case. The sound of footsteps grew louder. When she turned around, Barry asked, "Hate events like this, eh?"

Anne slowly nodded "yes," trying to picture where she had seen Barry before. Barry nodded in the direction of a nearby bench, motioning her to have a seat. Reluctantly, she sat down. Now she had no choice but to socialize. He mentioned that he recognized her from the time the young adult group served at the homeless shelter. Then he revealed that he totally identified with how she felt about being at group gatherings like this. He, too, used to feel the same way and made every attempt to isolate himself so he wouldn't have to talk with anyone.

Now Anne was listening. She was comforted that at least one person from that large group gathered inside understood what she was going through. He knew the range of emotions racing through her mind, adversely affecting her ability to interact with others.

As Barry began to express empathy for her, a hint of a smile crossed her face. When he asked her name again, she told him. Anne also blurted out that she had known Kristi, the event hostess, since high school. Barry said he could only imagine what it had been like for her when she spent time with Kristi, one of the most outgoing people he'd ever met. Anne laughed.

They reminisced about serving together at the shelter, and Anne slowly began to relax. Barry said if they walked back inside, she could stick by his side so she wouldn't feel alone. He did encourage her to socialize more often by taking advantage of the classes and fellowship opportunities their church offered. Doing so would ease the pain she was experiencing. As she became accustomed to listening to others, questioning them, and learning from them, she would become more comfortable doing so.

Anne had a feeling Barry was speaking from personal experience. She admired the ease with which he moved through the crowd, smiling and saying hello to others. She stood beside Barry as he talked with his friends. She watched how he approached each conversation, seeking to engage others and create relationships.

Over the next few months, Anne practiced Barry's techniques at each young adult event she attended. She smiled more, listened intently, and asked questions, taking 100% responsibility for connecting with others.

LISTENING LIFE APPLICATION CASE DEBRIEF

Anne accepted her friend's invitation to attend the party because she did not want to disappoint her. When Barry noticed that she was by herself on the patio, he approached and immediately began asking Anne questions. He related to how Anne must be feeling and engaged her in conversation to make her feel comfortable. He took 100% responsibility for how to most effectively approach Anne in an authentic and genuine way through emotional communication.

Based on his comments, she realized his intent was to empathize with her (emotional communication). As Barry was able to relate with Anne's feelings, she let down her guard a bit and felt more comfortable with him. He also engaged in persuasive communication as he invited her to stick by his side so she would not feel alone and also encouraged her to practice social communication.

Using the castle metaphor, Barry was able to get inside of the castle because he first engaged the guard (Anne).

CALL FOR ACTION: BUILDING BLOCK #3

✧ Be a responsible and responsive listener to God.

✧ Memorize the following verses:

  o *"Then Jesus said, "'Whoever has ears to hear, let them hear.'"* Mark 4:9

  o *"And lo, I am with you always, even to the end of the age."* Matthew 28:20

✧ Re-read the Parable of the Sower in Mark 4:1-20.

✧ From Pastor DeTellis' interview, identify at least 1-2 of his application points and put them into practice.

✧ Learn and apply the Five Purposes of Communication by taking 100% responsibility in all your relationships.

CLOSING PRAYER

Father, guide my listening to be Christ-like. Help me to listen responsibly and responsively to Your Word and to meditate on its meaning. I strive to honor You by using the talents You have given to me to communicate purposefully with You and all those whom You put on my path. In Jesus' name, I pray. Amen.

DITCH THE DISTRACTIONS

Martha, Martha," the Lord answered, "you are worried and upset about many things, but few things are needed—or indeed only one. Mary has chosen what is better, and it will not be taken away from her." Luke 10:41-42 (NIV)

Distractions are everywhere, just waiting to capture your attention. They also come in many forms, some more recognizable than others. One thing they all have in common is their ability to detract from your listening. The next *BE QUICK TO LISTEN* Building Block is Ditch the Distractions.

The lead scripture verse is from Jesus' visit to the home of the sisters, Mary and Martha. God knows you are easily distracted—with your time and attention pulled in many different directions. This reality sometimes leaves your prayers unfinished, your Bibles unopened, and your participation in worship sporadic.

The Christian-listener recognizes that the distractions in today's world play a major role in keeping him or her from being able to listen deeply to God's Word. You must take purposeful actions and exercise discipline to get rid of (or ditch) the distractions in your life.

BIBLE APPLICATION:
JESUS AT THE HOME OF MARTHA AND MARY

In the parable of Mary and Martha, Jesus visits their home. Martha works in her kitchen, distracted by all the preparations that often come with receiving guests; she has many tasks to accomplish. Her sister, Mary, however, is seated at the feet of the Master, Jesus. Martha is upset because Mary remains at Jesus' feet, listening to Him teach, while the burden of the chores falls entirely on her.

As Jesus and His disciples were on their way, He came to a village where a woman named Martha opened her home to Him. She had a sister called Mary, who sat at the Lord's feet listening to what He said. But Martha was distracted by all the

"Mary has chosen what is better and it will not be taken away from her."

preparations that had to be made. She came to Him and asked, "Lord, don't you care that my sister has left me to do the work by myself? Tell her to help me!"

"Martha, Martha," the Lord answered, "you are worried and upset about many things, but few things are needed—or indeed only one. Mary has

chosen what is better, and it will not be taken away from her." Luke 10:38-42

Martha's distractions are external. They are the chores, a "to-do list" she needs to accomplish before guests begin arriving at their home. Mary's distractions, on the other hand, are internal. She is thinking in her mind what Jesus will be saying or teaching while there.

Today, most people's lives mostly resemble Martha's— distracted by so many things— when the one thing needed is to listen to God. *("Be still and know that I am God"* Psalm 46:10.) This is what Mary did as she eliminated everything that distracted her, calmed her soul, and seated herself at the foot of her Master, eager to listen to Him.

To hear God's voice, it is important to develop the discipline of studying the Bible frequently, not only in your individual life but also with other believers. Moments of prayer, Bible study, and worship are occasions when you can especially listen to God. Anytime of the day or night offers an opportune time to listen and focus on Him. God is waiting to listen to you.

PASTOR'S LISTENING PERSPECTIVE

Reverend Bryan Chestnutt is the Senior Pastor of Grace Evangelical Lutheran Church in Durham, North Carolina. He has been part of the ministerial staff since 2003 and moved to his present position in 2007. Prior to that, Pastor Chestnutt served as Clinical Chaplain at University of

North Carolina (UNC) Hospital and Central Prison in Raleigh, North Carolina.

Christian-Listening is prayerful listening. It is a God-given ability and gift that we can listen to the truth in love, not just speak the truth in love. As a God-given ability, it's one we use with the help of the Holy Spirit. It's born of prayer and happens only as the prayerful Spirit says, "Open my ears to hear the truth you need me to hear," and to do so with love.

Christian-Listening is a spiritual discipline. "Spiritual" means it's from the Spirit and "discipline" means I have to learn it and keep on learning. I don't ever master it. The word "discipline" is related to "disciple," which means "to learn." It means "who I learn from" is important and not just that I learn how to do things.

In this world, it's ever more difficult to listen because there are so many distractions. I think it's so hard to be still and listen to God or anybody. If we're going to listen well, we have to have some time and some space, and we have to be together.

When I consider Christian-Listening, the following verses stand out for me:

- *"My sheep listen to my voice; I know them, and they follow me"(John 10:27). The most important listening that we do is first to God. I really do like the ancient tradition of baptism where the pastor would put the finger in the ear of the one being baptized and say, "Ephphatha!" (Greek for "be* opened"), which Jesus used when He healed the deaf man. God creates in us what was not there before in faith and that is the ability to hear His voice so that when we read Scripture, we're not reading, we're hearing. That's "thus hear the Word of the Lord."

- "Martha, Martha," the Lord answered, "you are worried and upset about many things, but few things are needed—or indeed only one. Mary has chosen what is better, and it will not be taken away from her." Luke 10:41-42 Jesus says, "This is the better part," to listen. The Greek word for listen is "akoúo." This is where we get the word "acoustics." and we're all aware of when there's good acoustics and bad acoustics. Some rooms are that way when there's a lot of noise around them. That's an acoustical problem.

- For the time will come when people will not put up with sound doctrine. Instead, to suit their own desires, they will gather around them a great number of teachers to say what their itching ears want to hear. 2 Timothy 4:3 I've always liked this passage with the idea of the "itching ear." There are things I want to hear that are not good for me, just like there's things I want to eat that are not good for me. So, I should be aware that my desires can tune my ear to hear things that are not good and pleasing; the passage says that the itching ear is the ear that has turned away from truth.

Here's what I want:" Give me a God-listening heart so I can lead Your people well, discerning the difference between good and evil. For who on their own is capable of leading Your glorious people?" (1 Kings 3:8-9) This is another Old Testament passage that says listening is a gift from God. I love that prayer from Solomon when God says, "What do you want?" I think when we're translating things like that, it's good to look at the Septuagint. The Septuagint is this very early translation from the Hebrew to the Greek. What the Septuagint says right there is that Solomon said, "Give to your servant a heart that is listening and discerning." That's what that really says. So, I think of that idea of the listening heart when I think of listening.

- *My dear brothers and sisters, take note of this: "Everyone should be quick to listen, slow to speak, and slow to become angry" (James 1:19). I find the practical advice in James really important, and I noticed you're using that as the title of your book. God has made us twice as able to hear than to speak, but we don't always think of it that way. We usually engage our mouth before we do our ears. I like also that James says we should be doers of the word and not listeners only. If I really listen to somebody well, it will change what I do.*

I think there are ways you can learn to listen. As far as professional pastoral training, I completed two years of clinical pastoral education in the hospital setting, which utilizes methods to record conversations and then to go over those reflectively with a group of fellow clergy.

So, I realized that there were echoes of transference I wasn't hearing—all kinds of things I was not hearing well. That helped me learn to listen better. Listening takes a lot of energy. I'm aware of when I'm listening to people. I may hear some things and file that away or later realize, "Wow, what did I really hear?" There are times when I'm listening that I don't have the energy to really engage where maybe I ought or need to do.

Listening is a gift from God. The most important thing is to listen to Him and to develop that life of prayer where you're able to say, "Help me listen." And also, where you're able to say, "God help me see the people You put in my path today. Help me see that I'm there to serve them and help me to see that serving them means not just telling them things but listening to them." A word I wrote down that I think is important is "attend" to them. I have to listen and observe to see what is happening in the first place.

When I was a hospital chaplain, I was sent to see a guy who had just been told he had terminal cancer, but he was being discharged. He hadn't told his family yet.

So, I went in with an agenda to determine which stage of grief he was in and walk him through two or three stages, or maybe even all five with him. I managed to get through none of those. It frustrated me that what he talked about was when he was young. He was in the Conservation Corps back in the 1930s and helped build some of our state parks.

I wrote the conversation I had with him verbatim, and just how he would not allow me to go to this place of facing,

"You're going to die soon." It was only after some other people helped me see that even though he had been told he was going to die, he was looking back with some pride and joy on some things he did. I was unable to listen and just celebrate with him because I had my own agenda. When I go in thinking, "This is what I'm listening for, or this is what I want to help the person speak about," that can be a dangerous, unloving, and ungraceful tactic.

Also, I don't know if this is true for most people, but my emotions can really impede my listening ability, especially if I'm feeling threatened or if I'm getting defensive. It depends on how we handle it, but as emotional tensions rise, and we get defensive, I think this really impedes our listening.

A growing issue for me is when people are really, really angry and out of control. Is listening something that can be helpful? Not always.

More recently, I've tried saying, "Okay, God, help me work really hard right now at listening because there's so much of me that wants to either get away from them or bark back at them.

I use a term that resonates a little bit more with Christian scriptures—"discern," or "God help me know what I am hearing." This is instead of assuming that I know what I'm hearing.

I think that humility is also dependent on God, and it's also like I don't need to know everything about this person but,

"What do you want me to know right now, God?" That humility and help is what I would call discernment.

I'm convinced that most electronic communication impedes our listening. It gives us the illusion that we're actually communicating better. I believe that the very best setting for listening is face-to-face because then you listen not only to words, but you listen to body expressions. You listen more to the tone of voice. You listen to facial expressions. Your ears and heart and all your senses work together to be part of the listening spirit and the listening heart.

LISTENING KNOWLEDGE

Distractions are everywhere, just waiting to capture your attention. A distraction is anything that interrupts SIER*—**S**ensing, **I**nterpreting, **E**valuating, and **R**esponding Appropriately (*stands for Memory). However, you have the power to reduce or eliminate distractions in order to focus on top priorities. This is why it's important for Christian-listeners to master the *BE QUICK TO LISTEN* Building Block, Ditch the Distractions.

The key to ditching the distractions is to understand what they are and apply a controlled focus. There are some distractions you can control, and some you can't. The challenge is to deal with the things that lie within the realm of your control.

You face two types of distractions: *internal*, or things that are in your mind, and *external*, or things in your environment. Examples of external distractions include all the noises like a phone ringing, a television, background music, and even other people's loud conversations. As many distractions exist as there are ways to be distracted. The biggest challenge is to learn how to convert the distractions that you believe you can't control into ones that are controllable.

The first step is to identify the distractions you deal with on a daily basis. Start with external distractions; they're the easiest to recognize.

What types of distractions do you deal with day-in and day-out in your life? How many times is your day interrupted by a ringing telephone? Do visitors frequently appear at your office door unexpectedly? In dealing with external distractions, like noises in the environment, it is important to place these into the category of things you can control.

So, while you may not be able to control the warm temperatures, you can control the way you respond to them and think about them. This becomes a very important exercise in self-discipline and self-leadership. You must practice self-awareness and, with the help of the Holy Spirit, control the numerous and constant distractions in your life. Make every effort to control them before they control you.

Internal distractions include daydreaming, jumping too quickly to conclusions about a speaker's statement, and engaging in mental arguments while the speaker is still trying to make his point. Emotions such as joy, excitement, anger, anxiety, sadness, or attraction are also internal distractions.

Remember, each distraction has the potential to create some type of cost, especially if it occurs repeatedly.

The opportunity exists for you to create a specific plan to overcome your internal distractions. One way to raise your awareness is to wear a rubber band around your wrist.

When you detect any type of internal distraction, simply snap the rubber band and force yourself to return to the moment. After all, you're in charge.

The Cone of Distraction[8]

Your physical location when you listen becomes very important in avoiding many distractions. Usually, distractions fade as listeners move closer to the speaker. Picture this Cone of Distraction in your mind's eye, with the speaker at the peak of the cone. The farther back the listener is in the cone, the greater the opportunity for disruptive distractions to occur. As you move closer, many distractions are eliminated.

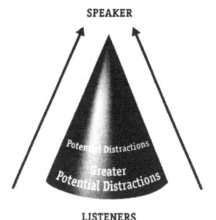

CONE OF DISTRACTION

SPEAKER

Potential Distractions

Greater Potential Distractions

LISTENERS

The Christian-listener always places God at the top of the cone by coming close to Him. Deeply listening to His Word and staying in His presence consistently will lead to a greater ability to successfully ditch the distractions in your life.

Multitasking Is a Myth

Many people pride themselves on how many tasks they can handle simultaneously. They truly believe that they are excellent multitaskers. Unfortunately, multitasking by humans remains a myth. While multitasking is a term taken from the computer field, computers don't actually do multitasking; rather, they do something called "task-switching"—doing one task at a time but very quickly. The same thing happens with humans.

The mind can manage only one thought at a time. So, when you're talking on the phone, checking your email messages, and trying to respond to your customers' requests—all at the same time—something is going to get ignored. It's crucial to slow down when going through the phases of the SIER* process. In other words, you need to slow down to go faster.

By doing one task at a time and giving each task your full attention, you'll get the tasks done more efficiently and effectively. When you try to do multiple tasks at the same time—and one or more of those tasks require you to listen—you are much more likely to miss key information, ask people to repeat themselves, or do an incomplete job. The end results?

You have to go back and fix mistakes you made because you weren't fully paying attention. In the long run, your efforts actually turn out to take more time.

At times, because of natural habits, listeners sabotage their listening success by introducing individual distractions to the communication process. There are five listening attention patterns: four that are negative and create mistakes, and one that is most effective. The dotted-line arrow represents a message being sent, while the solid arrow represents the listener's attention.[9]

In the first pattern on the next page, you see a small departure in the listener's attention. The listener is staying right with the speaker, but after an extended period of time, a small lapse occurs. In other words, the listener goes out for a short period of time yet returns quickly. This is the most effective pattern because you come back. You beat the distraction.

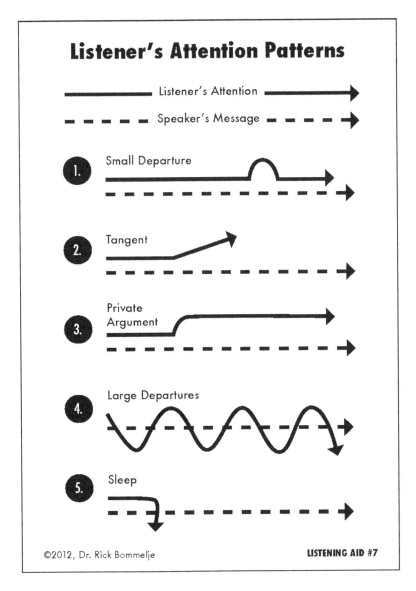

Listener's Attention Patterns

——————— Listener's Attention ———————▶

— — — — Speaker's Message — — — —▶

1. Small Departure

2. Tangent

3. Private Argument

4. Large Departures

5. Sleep

©2012, Dr. Rick Bommelje   **LISTENING AID #7**

In the second pattern—the tangent—the listener starts out with the best intentions but quickly goes off for an extended period of time. Hopefully, the listener eventually returns sometime later—or maybe doesn't. This pattern can create a cost because while you're "out," you may miss some valuable information.

In the third pattern—the private argument—the listener is challenged by the speaker's message in some way. Maybe he disagrees with the point being made. Instead of paying attention, the listener begins to prepare a defense in his mind. When the speaker completes her message, the listener launches into defending his own point of view.

The problem with this pattern is that while the listener is debating in his mind and preparing his defense, he is missing valuable information from the speaker; this information could help him understand the speaker and perhaps better inform his own position. This is another negative pattern.

The fourth pattern shows a series of large departures. Here, the listener is "out" more than "in." She is simply not paying attention to the speaker in the moment, though she thinks she is because she comes back periodically—though briefly each time. This pattern can produce a significant cost because the listener is relatively unaware of what is going on around her.

The fifth pattern is when the listener is zoned out so much that he actually falls asleep.

The challenge is to stay in the first pattern as much as you can for as long as you can. Doing this will help you to ditch the distractions. Distractions are so widespread and commonplace that people rarely take action to control or ditch them.

The main point of Building Block #4 is to compel you to stop tolerating distractions of any kind; in other words, you ditch them. The way to accomplish this lies in focusing on one thing at a time—and to know what matters most. This idea is simple to understand when you remember the "FOCUS" acronym:

Follow One Course Until Successful

LIFE APPLICATION

Ben glanced nervously at the massive clock on the conference room wall. His boss, Doug, was already 10 minutes late for their meeting. As each minute passed, his anticipation grew and his heart rate increased. He could hear the thump-thump of his heart and thought for sure you could see it jumping through his white, heavily-starched shirt.

Just as he was about to get up and leave, he heard the door open halfway. He could hear Doug's voice booming at the receptionist seated outside the conference room door. "I don't want to be interrupted," he stressed. Her reply, "Yes, sir," was barely audible.

Doug approached the table, and Ben stood up, extending his hand in greeting. Grumbling a few words, Doug sat down across from Ben. Doug then fumbled in his left pants pocket, retrieved a cell phone, and placed it on the table. Then he reached inside his right pants pocket, retrieved another cell phone, and placed the two side-by-side.

After clearing his throat and loosening his necktie, Doug stood up. "It's awfully hot in here," he said. "I've got to open some of these windows." As Ben shifted in his seat, Doug proceeded to open several windows and mumbled, "Ah, that's better."

Ben was anxious to get started. After all, he had no idea why Doug had summoned him up to the 3rd floor offices to meet. This was the first time Ben was privileged to gain admittance to the sacred flood of company executives. He remembered how shocked he was to receive Doug's message with the elevator code encrypted in it. Just as soon as he received it, he called his wife and told her about the meeting. She, too, was curious about why it had been scheduled so abruptly.

One of Doug's cell phones started to ring, and without excusing the interruption, Doug took the call. It was one of their clients who had reported a negative experience trying to get information from the Data Management Department. Only half listening to what the client was saying, Doug put the phone on mute and began talking to Ben.

"I've heard a lot of good things about your work, and I wanted to meet you in person," whispered Doug. Ben could hear the client rant and rave across the room. He managed to eke out, "Thank you. I've wanted to meet . . . "

Just then, the door to the conference room swung open, stopping Ben in mid-sentence. He had half expected to see the receptionist, but it was another woman—someone who works on this floor, he guessed, because he had never seen her before.

Trailing the woman were two children, whom Ben guessed might be around 7 and 5 years old. Then it hit him; this must be Doug's wife and kids. Doug, still with the cell phone plastered to his ear, waved her over to the table. He managed to introduce her to Ben and shared the names of his children, Lana and Deena. "Nice to meet you," said Ben.

Doug wrapped up the phone call with a promise to the client that he'd look into the problem and get back to him. He turned to his wife and asked her why she had come downtown to the office. "I thought we could have lunch together," she said. "The girls missed you since you have been out of town the past three days."

Ben looked up in disbelief. He didn't want to be kept in suspense any longer, and the thought of postponing the meeting while Doug and his family ate lunch was not how he had pictured this scenario. He was relieved when Doug asked his wife and daughters to wait in the reception area, telling them, "I'll be done in five minutes."

Five minutes? Ben was immediately taken aback by this statement. Why only five minutes? He figured that what Doug had to say to him must not be very important to only take another five minutes. The door slammed shut, and once again they were alone in the room.

By this time, a group of co-workers swarming into the next-door conference room lifted their voices in a rousing rendition of "Happy Birthday." When Doug got up to investigate, he saw several of his closest friends in the celebratory group and didn't hesitate to join the revelry. Ben stood watching from the doorway.

Doug looked up and saw Ben waiting. He was about to escort Ben back into their conference room when it dawned on him that he had promised to call his brother this morning. Here it was, approaching the noon hour, and he still had not made the call. Randy needed his advice on some decisions about their mother. Her health was deteriorating, and the brothers needed to decide how to best take care of her.

Motioning Ben to have a seat again, Doug rushed to the conference room table and picked up a phone. "I'll be right with you," he told Ben. "I just have to make this one phone call I'd promised to make earlier today."

Doug was talking to Ben as he moved to the other side of the room by the windows. "Let's get back to why I asked to meet you," he whispered to Ben as he waited for his brother to pick up on the other end. Ben could hear the phone ringing from where he was sitting and didn't bother to respond to Doug's statement.

Just then Ben heard a click on the line; someone must be answering Doug's call. He heard a female voice say hello. "Helena!" Doug said, "How great to hear your voice." From the sound of Doug's greeting, Ben knew this was going to be more than a brief conversation. He slumped down in his chair to wait again.

Doug was carrying on a conversation with his sister-in-law, Helena, in hushed tones. From the few words he could periodically recognize, Ben could piece together a skeleton of the matter at hand. He couldn't make out the exact reason for the conversation but kept hearing the words "money" and "dementia." Doug abruptly ended the conversation, and when he returned to the table, Ben could tell he was angry.

"Okay, Ben," Doug said. "Now let's get down to why I called you here." Ben thought he detected a sigh of relief in Doug's voice that indicated he was ready to finally talk. Ben's hopes soared.

"Finally," he thought.

"As I started saying earlier, I've been hearing good things about your work and wanted to meet you," Doug reiterated. His eyes began to tear up and, for a moment, Ben thought Doug was getting emotional. Suddenly, Doug began sneezing. Not once, but several times in succession.

Ben's eyes surveyed the conference room, hoping to find a box of tissues, and spotted one at the other end of the table; he retrieved it for Doug. As Doug dried his eyes, Ben walked over to the windows and abruptly shut every one of them. "Probably the grass pollen," he told Doug. From the tone of edginess in Ben's comment, it was easy to tell that the endless string of disruptions was frustrating him.

"Listen," Doug said. "I don't want to have to reschedule this. So, I'll get right to the point. The reason I called you here was to offer you . . ." He was interrupted by a very light knock on the conference room door. Ben couldn't help but roll his eyes. The door opened slowly, and a little blonde girl peeked inside. "Daddy, are you coming?"

"I'll be right there, Deena," Doug lamented. "Just a few more minutes." Ben was encouraged to hear that Doug was going to finish the conversation. The door closed but was too heavy for the little girl to shut completely, so it stayed cracked open a few inches.

"I called you here to offer you a new position. The job will be a lot more responsibility, and it's a promotion with a salary increase. Your supervisors have no doubt that you have the skills and determination to handle it." Ben did not catch the full essence of Doug's pronouncement as a disturbance outside the conference room indicated the two sisters were not getting along very well.

"Huh?" Ben asked. Doug got up and shut the conference room door, but not before admonishing the girls to keep the noise down. "I'm offering you a new position. There's an envelope on the receptionist's desk with full details. We're looking for you to start in two weeks, so you have the weekend to decide whether you want to take it. If so, you'll be moving up to this floor."

Doug stood up, and Ben followed. He extended his hand in thanks to Ben, who responded with a handshake. "I'll be expecting an answer one way or the other first thing Monday morning," Doug said as he exited the room, closing the door behind him.

Ben could not believe his ears. Here was the opportunity he and his wife had been praying for. He thought of calling her immediately but decided to look over the details of the offer first. When he got back to his desk and reviewed the paperwork, he was even more excited. Hurriedly, he put a call into his wife. She answered, and Ben began speaking so fast, she could barely understand what he was saying.

"Slow down," she said. "I think you're trying to tell me that a big promotion just came through. I want to hear all about it."

As Ben began to relay the story, he could hear the dog barking in the background. That could only mean one thing. Someone was coming to the door. Just then the doorbell rang, and the loud screams in the background told him that the baby had awoken from his nap. Ben took a deep breath. "Honey, you go get the door; I'll talk to you tonight when I get home." He ended the call and stretched back in his chair. Glancing up at the clock on the wall, he saw that almost three hours had passed since he left for his meeting with Doug.

Reviewing the events of the morning, Ben began to piece together why it had taken so long. The reason? Too many distractions had taken up the time allotted for the meeting. Ben realized he had just been taught a valuable lesson.

LISTENING LIFE APPLICATION CASE DEBRIEF

"Distracted Doug" violated all of the principles of Ditch the Distractions.

- ✧ Doug was multi-tasking and totally disconnected in the meeting with Ben.

- ✧ Doug was permitting both internal and external distractions to control him.

- ✧ In the process of meeting with Ben, he was unaware of the distracting signals he was sending to his employee.

- ✧ By allowing each new distraction to interrupt the meeting, Doug was disrespecting Ben.

- ✧ Doug was in the Large Departure attention pattern.

- ✧ Doug did not establish a distraction-free zone with others.

CALL FOR ACTION: BUILDING BLOCK #4

The Christian-listener recognizes that the distractions in today's world are what keep him or her from deeply listening to God's Word.

✧ Memorize the following verses:

   o *My sheep listen to my voice; I know them, and they follow me. John 10:27*

   o *"Martha, Martha," the Lord answered, "you are worried and upset about many things, but few things are needed—or indeed only one. Mary has chosen what is better, and it will not be taken away from her." Luke 10:41-42*

   o *For the time will come when people will not put up with sound doctrine. Instead, to suit their own desires, they will gather around them a great number of teachers to say what their itching ears want to hear. 2 Timothy 4:3*

   o *Here's what I want: Give me a God-listening heart so I can lead Your people well, discerning the difference between good and evil. For who on their own is capable of leading Your glorious people? 1 Kings 3:8-9*

✧ Re-read the story of Jesus at the home of Martha and Mary in Luke 10:38-42.

- From Pastor Chestnutt's interview, identify at least 1-2 of his application points and put them into practice.

- Identify your top listening distractions, both external and internal. Work each day at eliminating them.

- Put the Cone of Distraction into action in your life. Move closer to the speaker—and especially move closer to God.

- Stop multitasking. Instead, focus on what you are doing in the moment.

- Be mindful of the Five Attention Patterns and challenge yourself to stay in the Small Departure.

CLOSING PRAYER

Father, there are so many distractions in the world, internal and external, that keep me from learning and growing. Help me to stay focused and deeply listen to You so I can be shaped into the person You made me to be. Help me to practice Christian-Listening with those around me in the very best way possible. Be with me always and help me to be in Your presence throughout today. In Jesus' name, I pray. Amen.

LEAD YOUR EMOTIONS

"My dear brothers, take note of this: Everyone should be quick to listen, slow to speak, and slow to become angry." -James 1:19 (NIV)

The scriptural basis of the fifth Building Block centers on the title of the book, *BE QUICK TO LISTEN.* For centuries, wise men have warned of the dangers of being too quick to speak and too unwilling to listen. Poor listeners lose emotional control, usually quickly, and create conflicts and problems for themselves and others. Leading your emotions is one of the most difficult and important of the Building Blocks. It's a daily battle for the Christian-listener to be quick to listen to God's Word and eager to apply it in daily life.

When you have faith in Jesus Christ, the Holy Spirit lives within you and some of God's extraordinary virtues begin to become part of your life and guide how you live. The Bible calls these virtues "fruit," and they are evident in a life of trusting God for guidance. *But the fruit of the Spirit is love, joy, peace, patience, kindness, goodness, faithfulness, gentleness, self-control; against such things there is no law.* (Galatians 5:22-23)

As Christian-listeners, we seek to draw near to God, allowing Him to grow the fruit in our lives as we yield to the Spirit, the Comforter, Who guides us and helps us do the things God wants us to do—including being quick to listen.

BIBLE APPLICATION: *JESUS ARRESTED*

This is a universal teaching for all followers of Christ. In His Word, He urges us to "be in the moment"—that is, to be quick to listen. He then goes on to say that not only listening to the Word is important but being cautious and intentional with your response is as well.

In today's hectic world, all too frequently the standard operating procedure is just the opposite: it's be quick to speak, slow to listen, and quick to get angry at every chance you can!

This leads to painful costs, including hurt feelings, regret, and fractured relationships, just to name a few. When it comes to a relationship with God, you never reach a point in your life where there isn't a need to be quick to listen.

Judas came to the garden, guiding a detachment of soldiers...

> *When he had finished praying, Jesus left with His disciples and crossed the Kidron Valley. On the other side there was a garden, and He and His disciples went into it.*
>
> *Now Judas, who betrayed Him, knew the place, because Jesus had often met there with His*

disciples. So, Judas came to the garden, guiding a detachment of soldiers and some officials from the chief priests and the Pharisees. They were carrying torches, lanterns, and weapons.

Jesus, knowing all that was going to happen to Him, went out and asked them, "Who is it you want?"

"Jesus of Nazareth," they replied.

"I am He," Jesus said. (And Judas, the traitor, was standing there with them.) When Jesus said, "I am He," they drew back and fell to the ground.

Again, He asked them, "Who is it you want?"

"Jesus of Nazareth," they said.

Jesus answered, "I told you that I am He. If you are looking for Me, then let these men go." This happened so that the words He had spoken would be fulfilled: "I have not lost one of those You gave Me."

Then Simon Peter, who had a sword, drew it and struck the high priest's servant, cutting off his right ear. (The servant's name was Malchus.)

Jesus commanded Peter, "Put your sword away! Shall I not drink the cup the Father has given me?"

Then the detachment of soldiers with its commander and the Jewish officials arrested Jesus.

They bound him and brought him first to Annas, who was the father-in-law of Caiaphas, the high priest that year. Caiaphas was the one who had advised the Jewish leaders that it would be good if one man died for the people. John 18:1-14

Peter is someone who was close to Jesus and had been listening to Him during His entire ministry. Despite being by His Savior's side during Jesus' final years on earth, he does not fully understand why Jesus had to die. The "emotional" Peter pulls out his sword, wanting to prevent Jesus from heading down the road to Calvary. Something is preventing Peter from understanding who Jesus is and why He was sent here. Most likely, it's probably the same thing that prevents non-believers from understanding more about Jesus.

Peter is in the courtyard. All the other disciples have left Him alone, involved elsewhere in the controversy surrounding Jesus or hiding from it. He is embittered by the questions being thrown at him and engulfed by his fear. Peter's passion turns emotional, and these heightened emotions result in an angry reaction.

> *Now Peter was sitting out in the courtyard, and a servant girl came to him. "You also were with Jesus of Galilee," she said.*
>
> *But he denied it before them all. "I don't know what you're talking about," he said.*

Then he went out to the gateway, where another servant girl saw him and said to the people there, "This fellow was with Jesus of Nazareth."

He denied it again with an oath: "I don't know the man!"

After a little while, those standing there went up to Peter and said, "Surely you are one of them; your accent gives you away."

Then he began to call down curses, and he swore to them, "I don't know the man!"

Immediately a rooster crowed. Then Peter remembered the word Jesus had spoken: "Before the rooster crows, you will disown me three times." And he went outside and wept bitterly. Matthew 26:69-75

Picture in your mind's eye the scene in the courtyard. The precise moment of betrayal becomes carved indelibly into your heart. Just imagine Peter's grief when he realized that Jesus' prediction had come true.

PASTOR'S LISTENING PERSPECTIVE

The Reverend Dr. Wally Arp is the Senior Pastor of St. Luke's Lutheran Church & School in Oviedo, Florida. Prior to being called to St. Luke's in 1998, Dr. Arp was the pastor at Risen Christ Lutheran Church, Davenport, Iowa, for 10 years.

I think what's unique to Christian-Listening is the ability, in Christ, to be able to set yourself completely aside for the sake of the other person whom you're listening to. It is then rooted in the believer's ability to ground their sense of identity, their security, in Christ and what He has done for us on the cross—knowing that I'm a dearly loved, bound-for-new-heaven- and-new-earth child of the one and only Supreme Being in the universe, who sets me free to be truly present in the moment with another person.

In terms of related Christian-Listening scripture verses, I like to take it back all the way to the very beginning in the Creation account, where we hear: "In the beginning, God created the heavens and the earth" (Genesis 1:1), and He did so by speaking, by saying, "Let there be light and there was light" (Genesis 1:3).

In the Creation, words are the very power of God that create things, and then when God created Adam and Eve, He breathed into them the breath of life. Man became a living being, and He gifted humanity with an aspect of His own Divine image, which I think is perhaps manifested most clearly in our ability to speak and our use of words.

Jump forward to John, Chapter 1, Verse 1, and you get the same words, "In the beginning was the Word. And the Word was with God. And the Word was God. By Him all things were made, and without Him nothing was made that has been made." Then skip down to Verse 14, and it says: The Word became flesh and made His dwelling among us.

Our God is a speaking God, and words are one of the things that make us unique and distinct from all the rest of creation. To discuss our ability to communicate through words, both speaking and listening, I really like to start in the beginning.

The other is the Romans 10:17 passage that says: "Consequently, faith comes from hearing the Message and the Message is heard through the Word about Christ." Recognizing that if I'm going to be a listener, I have to be connected to Christ (which happens through this language phenomenon—the exchanging of words and hearing the words), that becomes the foundation for me of biblical listening.

I think that one of the biggest things for believers is being able to identify the noise that is going on inside of them that disrupts their listening. When I do premarital counseling with couples, I set up the communication diagram. I draw the sender and I draw the receiver, and then I draw the little squiggly line between the two of them and say, "Between those two, there's always noise." That noise can be the jack-hammer outside the window breaking up the sidewalk, but most of the time it's what's going on inside your own head—from how you're feeling, to what happened to you today at work, to how you were raised, to the whole sort of psychological phenomena of the way human beings have developed.

To be a good listener, you're going to have to learn to identify your own noise and reduce it so you can hear more clearly what other people have said.

I think the outcome of Christian-Listening is the other person feeling like they've been loved and that Christian-Listening is just always an "other-directed" activity that lets the other person experience the presence—your presence—with them in whatever it is that's going on in their life. I'm not sure how you measure that other than if they want to talk to you again.

People have to know that words are powerful things. They're probably the most powerful things that God has given to us. The old rhyme, "Sticks and stones can break my bones, but words can never hurt me," is absolutely wrong.

You should forget it and never say it again. Instead, insert "Sticks and stones can only break my bones, but words can pollute and destroy my soul forever." The first thing is telling people that words are powerful, and they can hurt. But on the flipside of that, words are what heal us.

That's why Christian counseling and therapy are so powerful. You have somebody who's willing to listen to you, and you can put what's going on inside of you into words. The very act of saying the words is part of the healing that you need.

My biggest struggle in communication and my listening relationship with my wife, Lois, is my defensiveness. For some reason, when she says things in a certain way without really meaning to or intending to, I hear her criticizing me or judging me, and that then sets off this defensive reaction in me that just kind of shuts down my ability to even hear what she's saying. During my extensive pre-marital counseling sessions with couples, my classic example is telling people I'm a workaholic. Work is my drug of choice. Work is what I use to make myself feel better. So, surprise! Surprise!

Over the years, Lois and I have had a struggle or two as to whether or not she and the children are as important to me as my work is. I came home from work one day and she said to me, "I mowed the grass today." And, I ask the couple then, "What do you think I heard based on the information I gave you previously?"

And most of the time they get it. "Oh, she was telling you that she had to mow the grass because you weren't home to do it, as usual." Which sets off all this defensive reaction in me. We've gone around that kind of conversation enough times to discover that what Lois is saying (if I try to actually use what I teach people to figure out what she's saying instead of assuming what she's saying) is that, "I mowed the grass today, and it'd be really nice if when you got home you noticed it and complimented me on it."

But what I heard was, "You're a jerk who never comes home and does what you're supposed to do and mow the grass," even though for 38 years I've known that she'd rather mow the grass than be inside cleaning. Passing through my *noise of being hypersensitive to her criticism and judgment of the phrase, "I mowed the grass today," sets off this whole cycle of argument that sometimes doesn't end very pleasantly.*

What I've learned from that over the years is that if you can't identify why you get like that, what the noise is in your own head, then you probably are trapped in a cycle that you can't get out of. What I discovered is that we tend to over-react to things that, for whatever reason, we have made the most important thing in our lives at that particular moment in time. So, what's the solution?

You have to root your identity in Christ, not in something else. To be a Christian-listener, you have to listen to God first. Then I think the daily discipline is when you get up every morning and remember who you are.

Martin Luther tied that to our baptism. Make the sign of the cross and say, "In the name of the Father and of the Son and of the Holy Spirit." Remind yourself through that recognition that in baptism you're connected to Christ— that your value, your character, your dignity, and your worth all come from God. That's the source then of your identity, which gives you that strength to be able to be a listener.

LISTENING KNOWLEDGE

Consider a time when you failed to listen carefully, simply because of your emotional reaction to the speaker. Maybe you disagreed with their political position or religious beliefs. Maybe you disliked their age, gender, or ethnicity. At what point did you stop listening? In many cases, your emotions got in the way.

Emotions are far-reaching. They affect everything you do, and it is important to take a broader look at your *triggers*. A trigger is anything that sets off an emotional reaction in you and disrupts your effectiveness as a listener. You react to three main types of emotional triggers:[10] (1) People triggers; (2) Topic triggers; (3) Language triggers.

Emotional triggers can be negative, but they can also be positive or just neutral.

You hold positive emotional views of certain people, topics, or sensations. When you are not aware of the power of such positive emotions, your listening becomes lazy. When you are emotionally connected to the speaker, the topic, or the way it's delivered, you may not bother to hear the complete message.

As you listen to your favorite subjects, to someone you admire, or to voices that appeal to you, whether you realize it or not, you enter your "emotional happy place." You may get a positive emotion from a person's physical appearance or by certain words that suggest powerful emotional images. These triggers provoke positive emotions in you that put your listening ability at risk; your "feel good" emotions bias your listening so you may not get the message. Without awareness, positive emotions can lead to ineffective listening habits and neutral emotions.

Neutral emotions also lead unknowing listeners to tune out speakers. While being neutral may provide an objective listening position, it can also be a trap. As emotionally neutral listeners create a position of disinterest, they simply drift out of the listening process.

Effective listeners, guided by the Holy Spirit, recognize the counter-productive impact of neutral emotions by identifying them and exercising discipline to overcome them. In the process, your focused listening interest and activity will be heightened.

Poor listeners lose emotional control in one or a combination of three specific areas: *speakers, words,* and *"hot" topics.* Once they are confronted with a person (or speaker) who upsets them, hear certain words, or consider a topic that riles them up, they react. The effect is usually negative. Some people quickly turn the reaction into anger. And any negative feelings and emotions toward the *speaker, words,* or *topic* will totally interrupt the listening process. In worst-case scenarios, negative emotions often lead to a refusal to listen. In addition, any attempt to listen with negative emotions usually results in angry listeners, and the evidence is clear: *mad listeners are bad listeners*.

The challenge is for you to be able to identify what the triggers are, be aware of heightening emotions, and slow things down so you can go through the steps of the SIER* process: **S**ense, **I**nterpret, **E**valuate, and **R**espond appropriately, with *Storing the event in your memory connecting the steps together. One example of this is "counting to 10" to keep from getting mad.

USE THE GOLDEN PAUSE

Let's put "counting to 10" into the language of listening. What you are really doing when you count is putting a space, otherwise known as the "Golden Pause," in the SIER* process, namely between the E and the R—a pause between your evaluation and your response. When you do this, you will be better able to control your emotions, and ultimately, respond in a way you choose. When you are able to do this consistently, you will develop a powerful spiritual discipline that will deepen your relationship with God and others.

"Thought," or thinking through a situation, is such an important part of behavior change—and something we can control if we choose to do so. For example, the following emphasizes the importance of thought:

I Am a Thought

I can make you rise or fall
I can work for you or against you
I can make you a success or a failure
I control the way that you feel and the way that you act
I can make you laugh, work, love
I can make your heart sing with joy, excitement or
elation, or
I can make you wretched, dejected, morbid
I can make you sick, listless
I can be as a shackle – heavy, attached, burdensome; or
I can be as the prisms hue, dancing, bright, fleeting, lost
forever
unless captured by pen or purpose.
I can be nurtured and grown and be great and beautiful,
Seen by the eyes of others through the action in you.
I can never be removed – only replaced...
I AM A THOUGHT – WHY NOT KNOW ME BETTER?

~ Anonymous

Know and remember these three steps that can help you lead your emotions in a positive, God-pleasing way:

Step 1: IDENTIFY YOUR TRIGGERS

- Mentally observe yourself in the moment.
- Gain more knowledge about the people, topics, and language.
- Label the triggers as positive, neutral, or negative, and determine why they are so.

Step 2: ANTICIPATE TRIGGERS IN YOUR CONVERSATIONS

- Prepare yourself mentally to encounter triggers.
- Decide on the preferred response.

Step 3: PRACTICE GAINING SELF-CONTROL THROUGH DISCIPLINED THOUGHT

- Intentionally interpret before making a judgment.
- Remind yourself that *you* decide your response.
- Before you respond, ask yourself, "Is it of value?"

With the help of the Holy Spirit, you will be able to lead your emotions. If you want to make a positive difference in your life and relationships, it requires stepping out in faith and conquering things that may appear impossible—doing things that may seem difficult at first. *("I can do all this through Him Who gives me strength."* Philippians 4:13*)*

These concepts are simple to understand, but the challenge is to remember them daily and use them consistently. The goal? *Intentionally respond* rather than *unintentionally react* to what you listen to every day.

LISTENING LIFE APPLICATION

When the phone rang and he glanced at the caller ID, Lee knew why Kim was calling. He tried whispering a brief prayer, asking God for guidance. The hurt from that painful Thanksgiving three years ago had shrunk but not disappeared. However, the thought of his sister waiting on the other end, almost 1000 miles away, shortened his conversation with God. He answered the call.

"Lee-Lee?" the voice on the other end asked. "Is that you?"

"Yes, Kim. It's me. You know how much I love you, but how many times have I asked you to stop calling me that? You know how it makes me feel."

"Oh, Lee, get over it. Forget about what happened. Don't keep going over old history. Come on home," Kim announced with a hint of lecture in her voice.

Lee was taken aback at Kim's response. He had expected sweet compliance to the request he just made to his younger sister, hopefully an apology for calling him by his much-dreaded nickname. This was a side of her he had never before experienced.

"I'm trying, Kim, I'm trying. Ten months of the year I'm fully committed to subjecting myself to another family gathering. Then, when the time comes to make the travel plans, I freeze up. I definitely miss all of you.

When I'm not there, I picture you all gathered around the table holding hands, heads bowed in a prayer of Thanksgiving. But that's where the happy scene ends."

Kim sighed deeply. She knew Lee was right. In fact, she secretly admired her older brother for standing his ground and not boarding a plane to their parents' home in the North Carolina mountains for the annual feast. Yet, on the other hand, her parents were aging, her children were growing, and the memories of times shared at the cabin were stronger. She missed her brother.

"Well, I guess you haven't started making flight reservations yet. Any day now, the cost of flights will increase—just in time for holiday travelers. If you call today, you might get in under the wire." Kim mentioned this merely as veiled incentive for Lee to make a commitment to attend. She knew that money was not an obstacle standing in his way. In fact, among the three siblings, Lee was the one who had done quite well for himself financially. She knew better than to mention finances to Lee for fear of re-opening old wounds.

Lee saw right through Kim's remark. "Don't get started again on the topic of money, Kim. I'm not going to discuss it over the phone or when we're all in the same room with each other, EVER again!"

By now, Lee's voice had taken on an angry tone. He didn't sound anything like the person who less than a minute ago had answered the phone in a kind, courteous voice.
Kim hesitated to continue the conversation. However, she had promised her dad that she would call Lee and do her best to convince him to come home for Thanksgiving. She couldn't let him down.

"Lee, you heard why I called, didn't you?" Kim asked. "I promised Dad I would reach out, try to smooth things over, and see if I could get you to change your mind this year. He really misses you, and Mom does, too."

At the mention of his mom, Lee fought every urge to hang up the phone immediately. If Kim were trying to make points with him, mentioning their mother was not the answer. In fact, hearing her name made him dig his heels in deeper. Now he would definitely stay home.

"If Mom wants me to be there, why doesn't she call me herself?" Lee asked. Deep down, he knew as soon as he saw her name on the caller ID, or heard the obnoxious ring signaling it was her, he would have let the call go unanswered. He saw no need to talk to her. Yes, time had passed, but Lee was realistic enough to know that her tongue would not be tamed, especially when it came to him.

"Lee-Lee . . . I mean, Lee," Kim replied, "Mom has had plenty of time to think about what she said. You might find it hard to believe, but she does have regrets about the hurt she caused. She's not very good at expressing how she feels. That's why she's distanced herself from you."

"Let me refresh your memory," Lee declared.

"No, Lee, you don't have to. Really, you don't," Kim pleaded.

"Well, I'm going to anyway," Lee resolved. Kim was his captive audience, and he half-cherished another opportunity to rehash the scene and re-establish his role as the victim.

Kim moaned. "Okay, Lee. I'll listen. But you have three minutes to talk, and then it's my turn. Fair enough?"

Lee started talking, and Kim was pretty sure he hadn't heard a word she had said. She stopped him mid-sentence.

"Lee, were you listening to me? Do you understand what I just said?" questioned Kim.

By Lee's silence, Kim knew he had not been paying attention to her. So, she repeated herself. "Lee, I'll listen to you for three minutes, and then it's my turn to respond. For the entire three minutes, I promise not to say a word."

"Oh, okay," said Lee, and he began weaving his tale of woe. Kim half expected him to apologize for not paying attention to her ground rules, but she knew her brother well enough to recognize that was unlikely to happen.

"She humiliated me in front of everyone seated around that table, Kim. Even though I responded to her insult with a light-hearted joke, the fact that she called me her 'inconsiderate son' was no laughing matter. Her comment cut like a knife, and I didn't see it coming. I left the room, gathered my belongings, and headed to the airport. I found out later that the comment stemmed from the fact that she and Dad had run into some financial issues a few months prior and I didn't offer to help them out. She never even asked if I was aware of what had happened. In Mom's typical style, she assumed I knew and then pronounced her sentence upon me for not meeting her expectations."

Kim indicated Lee's three minutes were up. Now it was her turn.

"Lee, that was the past, and let's no longer . . ."

Lee interrupted, "Don't lecture me again about putting the past behind us. Mom owes me an apology for embarrassing me and has had ample time to do so, and I've yet to hear even one word of remorse."

"Lee, it's my turn. I didn't interrupt you," Kim reminded him. "I've heard your story more times than I care to remember. Each time, I tell you how sorry I am that those words reached your ears. But I ask you to stop, pray, and think about how those words have consumed you over the past few years.

Obviously, your anger remains, and it dominates the feelings you have for the entire family. How do I know that? My girls haven't seen their uncle in two years! They don't know the details of the situation. All they know is that the uncle that took them on a pony ride has disappeared."

Kim let a few moments of silence pass by so what she had just said to Lee could sink in.
"Don't deprive your nieces of the chance to get to know you. They are the true victims here, not you."

Lee was left speechless and impressed at the same time. What an eloquent and impassioned plea from his younger sister! He had anticipated lots of guilt, crocodile tears, bribery, and even a free round-trip airline ticket to sweeten the pot. Nothing. None of that. Just words from his baby sister spoken from the heart. He was proud of the woman of God she had become and longed to give her a hug in person.

"Okay, Kim. You got me. How could I stand my ground with your little sermon? I'll make air travel arrangements this week. Tell everyone I'll be there."

Kim was elated. She couldn't wait to get off the phone and tell her daughters. They would be thrilled. Her next call would be to her dad. He, too, would be pleased. However, now his work was cut out for him. He had two months to convince his wife to seek reconciliation with their son.

LISTENING LIFE APPLICATION CASE DEBRIEF

1. Lee had a negative "people" trigger from his mother due to the incident at the Thanksgiving dinner two years ago.

2. Kim was keenly aware of Lee's pain and applied the Golden Pause by giving him the space to vent and share his feelings even though she had heard the same message multiple times.

3. Kim appealed to Lee to consider the bigger impact of him not having a relationship with his nieces and nephews.

4. Kim spoke from the heart, and Lee deeply listened.

5. Lee led his emotions and realized it was time to begin the healing process.

CALL FOR ACTION: BUILDING BLOCK #5

✧ Lead your emotions.

✧ Be eager to deeply listen to God's Word.

✧ Be intentional about responding and not reacting in all your relationships.

✧ Memorize the following verses:

   o *My dear brothers, take note of this: Everyone should be quick to listen, slow to speak, and slow to become angry.* James 1:19

   o *But the fruit of the Spirit is love, joy, peace, patience, kindness, goodness, faithfulness, gentleness, self-control; against such things there is no law.* Galatians 5:22-23

   o *Consequently, faith comes from hearing the Message and the Message is heard through the Word about Christ.* Romans 10:17

   o *Don't you know that all of us who were baptized into Christ Jesus, we were baptized into His death, we were therefore buried with Him, in order that just as Christ was raised from the dead, we, too now live a new life.* Romans 6:3

   ✧ Re-read the three stories about Jesus and his "emotional" disciple, Peter.

   ✧ From Dr. Arp's interview, identify at least 1-2 of his application points and put them into practice. Identify your triggers for each of the three categories: People, Words, and Topic. Work each day at recognizing and understanding them.

✧ You choose your response. Before saying or showing, ask yourself: Is it of value?

CLOSING PRAYER

Father, today I submit my mind, will, and emotions to You. Please forgive me for my outbursts of anger. I choose to lay down my sinful anger and accept Your mercy and grace. In the free will You have given to me, I choose to align myself with Your Word. Help me to live the fruit of Your Spirit and always listen first before I respond in ways that are pleasing to You. In Jesus' name, I pray. Amen.

TAKE MEANINGFUL ACTION

"Whatever you have learned or received or heard from me or seen in me—put it into practice. And the God of peace will be with you." Philippians 4:9 (NIV)

Listening is so much more than simply being silent, establishing eye contact, paying polite attention, and taking in the message. The listening process is completed with an *appropriate* response. The last Building Block emphasizes the necessity for the Christian-listener to take meaningful action. In Philippians 4:9, Paul exhorts us to follow his example by becoming doers of the Word. The Christian-listener's conduct is built on biblical content, and the outcome is to live a life that is God-pleasing.

BIBLE APPLICATION:
THE RICH AND THE KINGDOM OF GOD

As Jesus started on His way, a man ran up to Him and fell on his knees before Him. "Good Teacher," he asked, "what must I do to inherit eternal life?"

"Why do you call Me good?" Jesus answered.

He went away sad because he had great wealth.

"No one is good—except God alone. You know the commandments: 'You shall not

*murder, you shall not commit adultery, you shall
not steal, you shall not give false testimony, you
shall not defraud, honor your father and mother.'"*

*"Teacher," he declared, "all these I have kept since
I was a boy." Jesus looked at him and loved him.*

*"One thing you lack," he said. "Go, sell everything
you have and give to the poor, and you will have
treasure in heaven. Then come, follow Me." At this,
the man's face fell. He went away sad because he
had great wealth.* Mark 10:17-22

The fact that the young man approaches Jesus with his particular question suggests that he has already spent time listening to Jesus' teachings.

What are some clues from these verses that tell you this might be the case?

- ✧ The unnamed man calls Jesus, "Good Teacher."
- ✧ He knows about the gift of eternal life.

This rich young man starts out boldly by asking what he must do to inherit eternal life. Therefore, he comes to Jesus already committed to change. The decision was made. He wants eternal life.

He approaches Jesus with an open mind, expecting Him to fill it with the necessary steps he needs to take to reach his goal: eternal life. What the young man hopes to receive is a "to do" list of actions that he can check off and complete. To him, keeping the Law is merely showing outward signs of complying with the Law's requirements.

Jesus knows this. He has a different strategy in mind. The first step in His action plan is to refer the young man to something with which he is already familiar: The Ten Commandments. In particular, He mentions the seven commandments that prohibit wrong actions and attitudes against one's fellow man.

The young man's response, "All these I have kept since I was a boy," indicates that he could successfully apply his knowledge of the commandments. In his mind, he is actually doing what he is required to do.

The young man's earnest efforts reveal that he does not understand the spiritual depth of the commandments. His efforts lack inner obedience—they have not become second nature to him or part of his inner being.

Jesus implements Step Two of His action plan: He looks at him and loves him.

In Step 3 of His action plan, Jesus gets down to the heart of the matter. Knowing that the young man's primary problem is his wealth, He tells the young man exactly what to do in three steps:

1. Sell everything.
2. Give it to the poor.
3. Follow Him.

The young man fails to take meaningful action—to remove the obstacle that keeps him from trusting Jesus. He does an about face and walks away, turning His back on Jesus. He has a greater love for his possessions than he has for eternal life.

As the end of His action plan, Jesus uses His interaction with the rich young man as an object lesson to teach His disciples. He wants them to learn that the root of the problem for the young man is hardness of the heart. His unwillingness to abandon self and follow Jesus has eternal implications for him.

PASTOR'S LISTENING PERSPECTIVE

Pastor Joel Carl Hunter is the founding pastor of Northland, A Church Distributed, a congregation of 20,000 that worships at three sites in Central Florida and at more than 1,000 sites worldwide via interactive webcast, iPhone, and Facebook.

Christian-Listening is more than just being quiet while somebody else talks. It extends from praying that God will give you understanding as you hear throughout the day, to asking clarifying questions of people you are talking with, to feeling an affinity toward the person talking because you understand what they're trying to say. Christian-Listening is a matter of asking God to help you understand someone in a way that you, at least, are more empathetic toward them and, at best, have more understanding and maybe even a budding relationship or a better relationship with them.

The first discipline we have to practice is not reacting but tarrying long enough that you can form—not just an opinion—but also an appraisal. The scripture says, "But he who is spiritual appraises all things, yet he himself is appraised by no one." (1 Corinthians 2:15 NAS.) In today's world, the culture—the cultural trend—is just for immediate reaction, and mostly impulsive reaction. I think Christian-Listening is exactly the opposite; it means delaying any kind of response long enough that it can be an appropriate and accurate response. I think that's probably the main discipline we would have in this culture.

The Psalms are very good about identifying Christian-Listening. I will meditate on your precepts and consider your ways. (Psalm 119:15) Also, all the verses that have to do with being still and knowing God relate to Christian-Listening because of that stillness and listening for His instruction or His guidance.

There are scriptures that say, for example, in Luke 19:11: "While they were listening to this, he went on to tell them a parable, because he was near Jerusalem and the people thought that the Kingdom of God was going to appear at once." Jesus proceeded to tell them a parable. He had this art of not just dictating doctrine but really making listening a joy with his storytelling and inviting people to enter into the story. That's a different kind of listening.

The first one is listening to learn because you feel like you need to. The second one is really taking a journey with someone and, when I think of Jesus, how I still listen to Him through the scriptures. I'm taking a journey with Him, especially through the parables.

I've asked my congregation members to listen to someone for so long and with such reception that they could tell things from that other person's point of view—from that other person's perspective. They could not just repeat what the other person had said but do the kind of listening that puts them into the other person's mindset.

Part of the measurement of Christian-Listening is not only "Have I learned something?" but, "Do I feel closer to the person?" or "Do I feel like I at least understand the person and where they're coming from?" You are aware when you have that feeling, like "I really heard you." I'm not sure exactly though how you would measure it.

In his book, The Responsive Chord, *author Tony Schwartz said most communication is looking for a responsive chord in someone else (i.e., something that will help them respond on a gut level). The only time you're learning in a conversation is when you're listening. If you're in a conversation and you're not listening, you're not learning. If you're not learning, you're not growing. So, it's important that we prioritize listening.*

I learned to listen some time ago when an old college buddy of mine stopped by to see me. He was so excited because he had just been to this seminar on active listening. He sat down, and for an hour he never shut up about how to actively listen. Then at the end of this hour he said, "Oh, I've got to go. I'm on a timeline here. It was good to talk with you," and he just left. Here's a guy who wanted to tell me about active listening but not demonstrate any of it. I've always remembered that lesson.

Listening isn't trying to get your point across or trying to wait your turn so you can persuade somebody as to your own opinions. If you're going to listen, you've just got to really listen.

We live in a world of constant distractions, and they're only increasing (i.e., emails, texts, and the visual invasion of our focus that comes with constantly having technical accessibility).

We've got to become periodically inaccessible, or when we are in a conversation, make ourselves inaccessible to interruptions because there are very few people who have the discipline to ignore interruptions. It's a continuing art form—to prioritize a conversation or an endeavor where you're being taught about something— that you cut off the possibility of being interrupted from any but the most basic emergency.

I think the single most important behavior that the Christian-listener can develop as a daily practice is to ask questions, investigative questions, about what the speaker has just said. It does two things. First, it keeps you engaged so that you can really be listening in a way of retention.

But secondly, it helps you go deeper and get involved with the person in the conversation. It helps the other person feel valued, and I think that's very important for a Christian. We need to help people understand how valuable they are to us and how honored we are that they would be speaking to us.

LISTENING KNOWLEDGE

Taking meaningful action involves five important stages[11] that occur in a sequence of increasing mastery.

STAGE 1:

You have to ***commit***—decide to change. This means letting go of old ways and adopting new ones. It's a tough decision to make because being a Christian-listener entails taking the difficult road.

STAGE 2:

You have to ***know it***—open your mind to learn what to do. Listening—*really* listening—requires you to learn new ideas and new skills. This is knowing the 6 Building Blocks.

STAGE 3:

You have to ***do it***—act on what you know. This is the real test—practicing everything you know on a daily basis.

STAGE 4:

> When you've acted on what you know consistently over time, you can **be it**—you've made the practice of listening a part of your nature.

STAGE 5:

> The final stage is to **teach it**—you take what you've learned and pass the knowledge and strategy on to others. Teaching others how to listen accomplishes a number of things.

It keeps the concepts fresh in your mind, and it also reminds you to constantly set the example. But most importantly, it lets you help others become more effective communicators.

Aesop's Fable of "The Tortoise and the Hare" shows clearly what it means to take meaningful action.[12]

One day a hare was bragging to the other animals about how fast he could run. "I have never been beaten," he said, "for I am the fastest animal in the forest. I challenge any one of you to a race."

As he continued his arrogant boasting, he saw a tortoise standing among them. The hare laughed at the short feet and slow pace of the tortoise.

The tortoise stretched out his long neck and quietly said, "I accept your challenge."

"That is a good joke," said the hare. "I could dance circles around you the entire way." With a hearty laugh, the hare agreed to race the tortoise.

The forest animals met and mapped out the course.

On the fixed day, the race began. As expected, the hare left the tortoise far behind.

About halfway through the course, the hare decided that he had time to take a nap. "I have plenty of time to beat that slow-moving tortoise," he thought. And so, lying down under a shady tree, he fell fast asleep.

As for the tortoise, he never stopped for a moment. He took one good step after another, slowly and steadily plodding along.

Sometime later, the hare finally awoke from his nap. "Time to get going," he thought. As quickly as he could, he dashed to the finish line, where he met the tortoise patiently awaiting his arrival.

The moral of the story?
Slow and steady wins the race.

The rabbit was impatient and arrogant, and his attitude set him up for failure. He couldn't see the error of his attitude, how hurtful it was, and when it backfired on him, he lost the race. The tortoise, on the flipside, persevered throughout the entire race. He didn't give in to any distractions; he didn't let the rabbit push his hot buttons; and he stayed focused on the goal until victorious. This is how Christian-listeners approach every situation—and take meaningful action.

LIFE APPLICATION

Janine stared out at the sanctuary as the pews began to fill with members of her church. Only about 10 minutes remained until she was scheduled to address the congregation, and time was closing in on her fast.

She swallowed hard and looked for any familiar faces in the crowd. "There must be some of my friends here," she thought to herself. But, where were they? Glancing nervously at her watch, she figured they were either running late or not planning to attend. She wanted desperately to spot a familiar face.

A few members of the church's Executive Board made their way over to her. Several of them placed hands on her shoulder as a gesture of support. Perhaps they could sense the panic in her eyes and the tension mounting. Her fear made her very self-conscious, and she realized that her shoulders were hunched up in nervous anticipation.

Since agreeing to serve as Congregation President, Janine had dreaded this day—the first time she'd have to stand in front of her faith community in an open-forum question-and-answer session. She had to admit that since becoming Congregation President, God always seemed to send the right people at the right time to support and encourage her. She never felt alone or abandoned—not for one minute.

For this, she whispered a prayer of thanks. While she was at it, she decided to tag on a prayer for strength to get through this congregational meeting.

Looking up from her folded hands in her lap, she saw the sanctuary almost filled to capacity. The front rows, now no longer vacant, were always the last ones to be taken. "Meetings are no different than Sunday morning worship services," she thought to herself.

Janine moved to the first pew and took an aisle seat. This way, when it came time for her to talk, she need walk only a short distance in the silence. Every second she took to approach the microphone would be one second more she'd worry about her upcoming responses to the questions at hand.

The President-elect of the congregation, Mike, opened the meeting with prayer and then asked Pastor Ryan to explain the procedure for asking a question. He instructed those wishing to speak to step up to the microphone, present their question to the Congregation President, and then remain at the microphone until the answer had been given. Pastor Ryan then emphasized the importance of respect and courtesy for those speaking and that this was a perfect opportunity to practice their listening skills.

Listening skills! Janine's ears perked up as she heard those two words. Allowing a trace of a smile to cross her face, Janine began to recall the course on Listening Skills offered through her job a few weeks ago. "If I can remember those strategies and put them into action, maybe this congregational meeting won't be so bad after all," she mused. "In fact, it might turn out to be an ideal place to put into practice what I learned."

Janine realized that Pastor had invited the first speaker to approach the microphone. She stood up and worked her way to the front of the sanctuary, picked up the handheld microphone, and smiled. She spoke a few words of welcome and then encouraged the first speaker to pose a question. By that time, a word had popped into Janine's mind: SIER*. That was the strategy she most remembered from the listening course.

Making every effort to be present in the moment, Janine glanced around the room to take in her surroundings. She caught sight of the church's stained-glass windows, picked up a gentle scent from the roses on the altar, savored the remnants of a breath mint, and prompted the speaker to begin.

With a hint of timidity, the speaker apologized that his question would have several parts. Janine encouraged him to keep speaking. As he talked, she maintained eye contact with him and fought the urge to interrupt or jump to conclusions about why he was posing this particular question. When he finished speaking, Janine's turn to respond had arrived.

Janine asked a few questions to clarify that she understood the speaker's question. Almost intuitively, she decided to summarize the question for the audience's benefit. Right now, however, Janine was having a difficult time keeping her emotions in check. She had interpreted portions of the question as criticism and wanted to immediately react, rather than respond.

Instead, she contained herself, maintained eye contact with the speaker, Larry, ignored her personal thoughts, and spoke clearly and confidently to his question. When Janine had completed her answer, she asked Larry if her response had satisfactorily answered his question. He nodded affirmatively and returned to his seat. The next speaker approached the microphone.

Janine's heart skipped a beat when she looked up and saw who was standing in front of her. Bill was a charter member of the church; his family was responsible for starting the church close to 75 years ago. Over the years, Bill's family had been ardent supporters of the mission of the church—both financially and with their time and talents. Janine knew almost every member of Bill's family, and even among his relatives Bill had a reputation of being stubbornly resistant to any changes taking place in the church. She took a deep breath, whispered a brief prayer, forced a weak smile, and greeted Bill.

Janine tried not to guess what he was going to ask. She wasn't quite as worried at the question he might present as she was about the complaints and criticisms she knew he had stored up. She took a deep breath and encouraged Bill to begin. Under her breath, Janine asked God for strength and focus as she waited for the shoe to drop.

Bill cleared his throat before uttering a single word. He looked around the sanctuary and then directly at Janine. "Miss Janine, I would like to say a few words. When you were elected President of this congregation, I had my doubts about whether you would be able to stand up to all the shenanigans that go on around here." Janine smiled as the congregation managed to generate a hushed laughter.

"But after today and the way you handled some of those tough questions coming at you, I have no doubt that you will do just fine. Your answers were right on, and all of us watching were witnesses to what a skilled listener you are." Just then, a voice boomed from the congregation, "Wait, I want to say something."

Bill turned around in an attempt to locate the voice's origin. He saw it was his cousin, Jim. "Jim, haven't you learned anything by listening to Miss Janine? Never once did she interrupt the speaker like you're doing right now." This time, the laughter from the congregation grew louder. A smile came over Bill's face.

Janine quickly thought back to all the times she had seen Bill and could not recall a single instance when he was smiling. "Cousin Jim," Bill said, "I've wanted to say that to you for a long time. Please stop interrupting people when they're speaking. Let the person finish before you jump in. Haven't you been watching Miss Janine for the past hour and a half?"

"Yes, I have," said Jim. He slowly lowered himself into his seat. Janine noticed the ear-to-ear grin on the face of Jim's wife, Joyce. It almost looked as if she were happy that someone had finally addressed her husband's disruptive nature. God only knew how much she had tried to do the same thing.

"Miss Janine," Bill said, "thank you for showing this community of faith how good listening skills prove vital and effective to us all. At the end of the day, we all should recognize that listening is essential to our faith and even for others to come to faith in Jesus Christ. If you don't believe me, just look up Romans 10:17: *"Consequently, faith comes from hearing the message, and the message is heard through the Word of Christ."*

By this time, almost every person in the room had an astonished look on their face. They had never seen or heard this side of Bill. His words seemed totally out of character and would have been dismissed as nonsense except that he was convincingly sincere.

"Miss Janine," Bill continued, "while I watched you listen, that Bible verse from Romans just popped into my head. Then, it dawned on me! We all have a choice to listen to the Word of God or not. We all know where we will wind up if we keep ignoring what God has to say or denying what He says. Death. However, if we would just pay attention to the life-giving qualities of the Word of God, we'll wind up in a different place. It's pretty simple: Be Quick to Listen.

Janine rose to her feet and joined the congregation's applause. She let out an enormous sigh of relief and couldn't help but notice the smile on Pastor's face. The Holy Spirit had used Janine's listening skills to soften Bill's heart. Pastor Bryan gave Janine a thumbs-up. If only Janine knew about his epic attempts to reach Bill's heart and soul with God's Word. This time was different. God spoke, Bill listened, and his life was transformed.

LIFE APPLICATION CASE DEBRIEF

1. Even though she was apprehensive during this first congregational meeting, Janine led by her listening.

2. Janine applied the listening knowledge that she learned in the class.

3. She remembered SIER* and put it into immediate practice.

4. Janine modeled the way for the congregation as she respectfully received each comment and question.

5. Even though she was aware of Bill's aggressive personality, she welcomed him and was eager to receive his message.

6. Bill noticed and named the listening behaviors that Janine was practicing during the meeting.

7. Bill directly connected Janine's listening behavior by lifting up the Romans 10:17 verse.

8. Bill was practicing Christian-Listening and spoke with conviction about the effectiveness of Janine's listening leadership actions.

CALL FOR ACTION: BUILDING BLOCK #6

✧ Practice the five stages of "Take Meaningful Action."

✧ Respond *appropriately.*

✧ Memorize the following verses:

   o *Whatever you have learned or received or heard from me or seen in me—put it into practice. And the God of peace will be with you.* Philippians 4:9

   o *But he who is spiritual appraises all things, yet he himself is appraised by no one.* 1 Corinthians 2:15 (NAS)

   o *While they were listening to this, He went on to tell them a parable, because He was near Jerusalem and the people thought that the kingdom of God was going to appear at once.* Luke 19:11

   o *Consequently, faith comes from hearing the message, and the message is heard*

through the Word about Christ.
Romans 10:17

✧ Re-read the stories of the Rich Man and the Kingdom of God. (Mark 10:17-22)

✧ From Dr. Hunter's interview, identify at least 1-2 of his application points and put them into practice.

✧ Periodically, read Aesop's Fable, "The Tortoise and the Hare."

✧ Notice when you are intentionally practicing Christian-Listening and the outcomes you receive.

CLOSING PRAYER

Lord, you have equipped me with the knowledge and skills to practice being a Christian-listener. Help me have the presence of mind to always deeply listen to You first. Guide me in my thoughts, words and actions in every listening situation I encounter. In Jesus' name, I pray. Amen.

CONCLUSION

"But the one who listens to Me will live in security and will be at ease from the dread of harm." Proverbs 1:33 (NET).

The Book of Proverbs communicates an abundance of wisdom using a scarcity of words. This simplicity, the form Solomon uses to convey his thoughts, does not take away from the depth of meaning contained in each verse. They are words of a teacher offered to save the young and inexperienced from the slower and more painful process of learning by experience.

Like a father giving instructions or a mother lovingly guiding her children, Solomon offers knowledge and counsel in an attempt to keep children from straying. Knowing that temptation is evident, evil is widespread, and danger is looming, wisdom is the voice of the Heavenly Father instructing His human children and shepherding them into a happy and prosperous life.

Within the Father's unmistakable and persuasive voice is a warning and an assurance. To ignore God's wisdom brings ruin. To seek it brings security and peace. Wisdom, however, is helpless unless its voice reaches our heart and echoes in our soul. Consequently, when wisdom lifts its voice, the children of God must hear it.

BIBLE APPLICATION:
TEACH YOUR CHILDREN WELL

In the Old and New Testaments, God repeatedly stresses the importance and value of teaching children. In the Old Testament, the Books of Deuteronomy, Psalms, and Proverbs are instructive to God's children, young and old alike.

"All your children will have God as their teacher – what a mentor for your children!"

"All your children will have GOD for their teacher what a mentor for your children! You'll be built solid, grounded in righteousness, far from any trouble—nothing to fear! far from terror—it won't even come close!" Isaiah 54:13-14 (MSG)

Deuteronomy is directed to the children of Israel; and many of the Psalms teach forgiveness, divine mercy, and repentance; and Proverbs teaches wisdom and knowledge, especially to young men.

Timothy, who accompanies Paul on his missionary travels, was taught by his mother and grandmother (2 Timothy 1-5). In the Gospels, Jesus openly demonstrate His love for children. He takes time to hug and hold them and asks God to bless them. Matthew, Mark, and Luke all write about Jesus' harsh words of criticism to His disciples for trying to keep little children away from Him. He knows that children are humble, teachable, willing, and eager to learn, more likely to simply take God at His Word.

PASTOR'S LISTENING PERSPECTIVE

Pastor Debbie Stanley, Ph.D., serves as the evangelist at Grace Christian Fellowship in Little River, South Carolina. She oversees the Children's Ministry at Grace, as well as stands in the pulpit at various times throughout the year. She retired in 2012 after dedicating 32 years of her life as a public-school educator and Early Childhood professor at the University of South Carolina and Coastal Carolina University.

To me, Christian-Listening involves listening to the deeper realm of God's voice and how it shows up in the voices of other people. But you've got to really listen deeply to others to hear it. It's like listening for the sound of the Divine, which, I believe can flow to people through the preaching of the Word and through the singing of the Word. It's the mindful and very heartfelt, very soulful listening to God and to others. It's not a general conversation. When I'm thinking about times I hear God's voice, I'm thinking of my prayer time and how we come out of that time listening to and receiving teaching from the Divine, from the Voice above, in whatever form it will show up.

Christian-Listening takes root through faithful practice. First of all, define it for yourself and lean into that definition and see what emerges. When I'm working with children, not only is it my spiritual path but also it is my vocation. I listen for God's voice through children. I think they are His voice in its purest form because it's an open and honest discussion with children. They're just there and raw. I find that listening to children is what I love about my role as a children's pastor.

Also, another practice is being very intentional with how I'm listening, especially in my prayer time—my quiet time. For me, it also happens during my times of walking on the beach, especially when I'm struggling to know what direction I need to take.

When I think about listening in the scriptures, I like the way Jesus asks questions to those of us followers. In the New Testament, when Jesus asks His disciples, "Who do men say that I am?" (Matthew 16:15). He's asking an open and honest question, and yet He continues to build on what they're saying. Then finally, He creates such an open space. Peter said, "Thou art the Christ." (Matthew 16:16). Jesus simply led them by listening to their responses and building upon that to get to this Divine revelation.

Another scripture verse was when Peter denied Jesus, and Jesus asked, "Peter, do you love me?" (John 21:17) He continued to ask him that and let Peter hear himself more deeply. Those are the two that stand out in the New Testament for me.

Moses, Jeremiah, and Job all had deep conversations with God while they were in horrific conditions. But that deep listening to His voice and yearning to hear and to know brought such a peace—a profound peace that sustained them through the most dark and dreary hours and allowed them to trust in the divineness of God over the situations they were in.

I believe that God knows everything. He asks those honest questions of us to open us up. When I define it as a Christian, it is an honest question from the Divine that opens me up in my humanity to better receive that from the Divine that which I need for any given situation. When I ask questions, I'm really praying and seeking deeper listening to God for the question that will really help the person open up to their own inner truth and their own inner teacher. I think those questions that I receive when I open myself up to the Divine allow me to ask the questions of the others whom I'm around that are as open and honest as I may sense.

For my congregation members, in helping them learn the importance of listening, I teach them prayer. I encourage them to go to prayer and then choose silence to listen to the Divine and put their requests out there. Jesus told us very clearly to let your requests be made known to God who knows all things anyway. (Philippians 4:6)

I call it practicing in the presence of God. This is listening in the most natural places, like when I'm doing the dishes. This is practicing presence. When you're practicing presence, it's listening in the most mundane tasks of everyday living and listening deeply for the Divine. Wherever I go in my interactions with others, I'm listening and making it a daily practice that I practice in the presence of God—every day. And I encourage the parishioners in our church to do the same. I teach an entire 12-week course each year for new members on practicing presence.

One of the main distractions that prevents Christians from effectively listening today is anxiety. It's the mentality of not having enough time and trying to isolate prayer from their everyday lives. They may think, "Okay, I'm going to get 10 minutes of prayer in right now because I now have enough time." They could pray all day.

I breathe; therefore, I pray—just soaking in, knowing that God is everywhere. I love to designate my time in the day to really wake me up into the fullness of the blessings that He has laid out for me today—paying attention to all my experiences today and when I close the day, my goodnight prayer, remembering these wonderful opportunities I had to see the Divine in action.

So, practicing presence is just walking through my daily life, the people I meet, the experiences I have, with the intentionality of finding it as a gift from the Divine this day. Give us this day our daily bread (Matthew 6:11). On this day, I want to "munch it." I want to get every morsel out of it that I can on being mindful and intentional about practicing presence. Fear or anxiety take away from the wealth and the abundance that's right before me. His way is made for us. His way is always available. It's just a matter of paying attention. If you allow fear and anxiety, you cannot pay attention to what's unfolding right before you.

LIFE APPLICATION

Deondre was about to step into new territory; he was about to walk into the junior high Sunday School classroom as the teacher for the very first time. He had never taught Sunday School before and was excited to use his gift of teaching, especially with students in this age group. As a corporate trainer for a large manufacturing company, he worked hard to clearly explain concepts, principles, and techniques in ways his participants could understand and implement on the job. He also prided himself on his ability to fully engage a group. Halfway down the hallway, Deondre looked ahead and spotted his friend, Zack.

Zack had served as a Sunday School teacher for the past five years, but since he and his family were relocating across the country, he had recommended that Deondre take over the class. Deondre had immediately accepted the offer.

As the two men approached the open classroom door, the students' voices grew so loud that Deondre thought some of them might even be fighting. Although the men stood in the doorway to announce their arrival, no one noticed them. Zack coughed loudly.

A few students looked up and immediately began to nudge those who were still talking; they nodded towards the door to signal their new teacher's arrival. Several students in the class recognized Zack as their teacher from a previous class and greeted him with shouts and squeals. Apparently, they assumed he was going to be their teacher this year. As soon as Zack introduced Deondre as their official teacher, the decibel level spiked up again as the students returned to conversing with each other.

Deondre greeted the class; however, his words were ignored. He tried again, this time raising his voice to drown out the noise in the room. Still no success. Zack smiled, turned around, and left the classroom. Deondre was alone with 10 seventh- and eighth-graders.

There were six boys and four girls gathered in small groups around the room. As Deondre took inventory of the clusters of students before him, one girl standing with a group of other girls noticed him. She began elbowing her friends, who, in turn, caught the attention of the other students. The noise died down, and, heads were finally turned toward him. He smiled, introduced himself, and asked the students to find a seat. With no sense of urgency, they made their way over to the round tables.

The volume level increased as students began calling to each other to sit at the same table. Deondre tolerated the noise briefly and encouraged the students again to sit down. This time he raised his voice noticeably and added another invitation: "Ladies and gentlemen, please be quiet so we can begin." They finally listened and complied.

Deondre informed the students that they would begin each class with a prayer. Trying to turn his comment into a teaching moment, he reminded them that prayer was God's way of deeply listening to His children and that, in the silence of prayer, they had the opportunity to hear God's voice. Beginning each class with prayer, similar to beginning each day with prayer, was a positive foundation for their lives, he told them.

Heavenly Father, we gather together to learn and grow from Your wisdom. Help us to become ready to receive the lesson You have for us today. We hunger for Your truth and seek You first. We surrender every part of our lives to You. In Jesus' name we pray, Amen.

After the prayer, Deondre introduced the Bible lesson. "This week's lesson is about the story of God calling the prophet Samuel," Deondre began, and he continued reading aloud:

Now Samuel did not yet know the LORD: The Word of the LORD had not yet been revealed to him.

A third time the LORD called, "Samuel!" And Samuel got up and went to Eli and said, "Here I am; you called me."

Then Eli realized that the LORD was calling the boy. So, Eli told Samuel, "Go and lie down, and if He calls you, say, 'Speak, LORD, for your servant is listening.'" So, Samuel went and lay down in his place.

The LORD came and stood there, calling as at the other times, "Samuel! Samuel!"

Then Samuel said, "Speak, for your servant is listening."

And the LORD said to Samuel: "See, I am about to do something in Israel that will make the ears of everyone who hears about it tingle."

The Lord came and stood there, calling as at the other times, "Samuel! Samuel!" Then Samuel said, "Speak, for your servant is listening."
1 Samuel 3:7-11

Deondre looked up from the Bible and made eye contact with each of his students. He repeated verse 10: *"Speak, (Lord), for your servant is listening."* and then let silence fill the room.

"How many of you have taken a listening class in school?" he asked. No hands went up. "We don't need to take a class on listening because we do it all the time," one student exclaimed. Deondre asked a second question: "Who in the room has ever felt like others weren't listening to you?" All hands shot up. "And how did that make you feel?" The students called out a litany of descriptive words: "hurt," "misunderstood," "angry," "confused," "alone," "not taken seriously," and on and on.

"Exactly!" exclaimed Deondre. "Samuel was ready to listen to God. Are you? "Do you know how?" More silence ensued.

Deondre held their rapt attention. "During our six weeks together, we will be focusing on how you can listen better to God and to each other. Being a better listener has helped me in all areas of my life, especially as a Christian. I teach a short course on listening at my workplace and I'll share with you practical ways that you can become a better listener at home, at school, and here at church. But most important, the Bible includes over 2,000 verses with the words 'listen,' 'listening,' 'hear,' or 'hearing.' We will connect the Bible and listening knowledge together." In closing, he projected a scripture verse on the screen and asked everyone to read it out loud together:

My sheep listen to my voice; I know them, and they follow me. John 10:27

The students seemed interested in what Deondre had to offer, bringing him a huge sense of relief. One student asked him what the name of the class was going to be. Deondre smiled and stated:

"BE QUICK TO LISTEN."

Heavenly Father, help us to live by Your words in James 1:19 that we Be Quick to Listen. Lead us to learn how to deeply listen and how to best listen to You and to Your responses to us. We know through Your Word that listening is a spiritual discipline that You give to us. Open our ears, our minds, our hearts, and our souls to learn how to be Christian-listeners. Teach us the wisdom of Your ways so we can walk with You and experience every blessing You have for us. In Jesus' name we pray, Amen.

ENDNOTES

Introduction

[1]Adapted from the six listening strategies. Bommelje, R. (2013). *Listening Pays: Achieve Significance Through the Power of Listening*. Orlando, FL Leadership & Listening Institute, Inc.

Chapter 1

[2]Adams, G.W. (1914) *Listen.* The Daily Evening Journal, Pittsfield, Mass.

[3]Adapted from the 10 Golden Rules. Steil, L. and Bommelje, R. (2004). *Listening Leaders: Ten Golden Rules to Listen, Lead and Succeed.* Edina, MN: Beaver's Pond Press, pp. 41-50

[4] SIER* created by Dr. Lyman K. Steil. Steil, L., Barker, L., and Walston, K. (1983) *Effective Listening.* New York: McGraw-Hill College.

Chapter 2

[5] Steil and Bommelje, 2004, Ch. 3., pp. 75-99.

Chapter 3

[6] The Four Soils. Bible.org. https://bible.org/seriespage/3-four-soils-matthew-131-23-mark-41-20-luke-81-15.

[7]Bommelje, 2013, Ch. 14, pp. 151-157.

Chapter 4

[8] Steil and Bommelje, 2004, Ch 7., p. 229.

[9]Adapted from Coakley, C. (1993). *Teaching Effective Listening: A Practical Guide for the High School Classroom.* Auburn, AL: Spectra, Inc.

Chapter 5

[10] Bommelje, 2013, Ch. 16, p. 203.

Chapter 6

[11] Bommelje, 2013, Ch. 17, p. 217.

[12] Bommelje, 2013, Ch. 17, pp. 214-215.

ABOUT THE AUTHORS

Rick Bommelje is a 'Listening Seeker' and teaches what he needs the most help in. He serves as a Professor at Rollins College in Winter Park, Florida and guides learning journeys on listening and leadership at the undergraduate and graduate levels. He is also the founder of the non-profit organization Listening Wisdom, Inc. that exists to help the world listen better. Rick is the author of *Listening Pays: Achieve Significance through the Power of Listening* and co-authored the pioneering book with Dr. Lyman Steil, *Listening Leaders: The Ten Golden Rules to Listen, Lead, and Succeed.* He is a lifetime member of the International Listening Association, a Certified Listening Professional, and was inducted into the Listening Hall of Fame.

Christine T. Wethman is a 'Listening Student' who continues to learn the value and significance of listening in her life and faith. She graduated from the Weatherhead School of Management, Case Western Reserve University in Cleveland, Ohio with an MS in Positive Organization Development and Change. After retiring from serving in ministry for 18 years, Chris, an Appreciative Inquiry Practitioner, now devotes her time helping churches with visioning and strategic planning. She has authored the book – *The Good News According to Rock-n-Roll: Commentaries on Rock-n-Roll and Folk Songs to Strengthen Your Christian Faith.*

FACILITATOR'S BIBLE STUDY

Download your free *Be Quick to Listen*
Facilitator's Bible Study

at

www.bequicktolisten.com

To contact us directly,

Rick Bommelje   Christine T. Wethman

rick@bequicktolisten.com   chris@bequicktolisten.com

LISTENING RESOURCES

A non-profit organization that serves as a clearinghouse for practical and relevant listening resources including books, articles, instruction, TedTalks, organizations, podcasts, and many others.

www.listeningwisdom.org

100 BIBLE VERSES CONTAINING THE WORDS: *LISTEN, HEAR, HEARD, HEARING*

Key to Bible translations:

CSB = Christian Standard Bible

CEV = Contemporary English Version

ESV = English Standard Version

ISV = International Standard Version

KJV = King James Version

MEV =Modern English Version

MSG = The Message

NAS/NASB = New American Standard Version

NCV = New Century Version

NIV =New International Version

NLV = New Life Version

TLB = The Living Bible

1. Now therefore, my son, **listen** to me as I command you. Genesis 27:8 (NASB)

2. God **listen**ed to Leah, and she became pregnant and bore Jacob a fifth son. Genesis 30:17 (NIV)

3. Then God remembered Rachel; he **listen**ed to her and enabled her to conceive. Genesis 30:22 (NIV)

4. "Assemble and **listen**, sons of Jacob; **listen** to your father Israel." Genesis 49:2 (NIV)

5. But Moses spoke before the LORD, saying, "Behold, the sons of Israel have not listened to me; how then

will Pharaoh listen to me, for I am unskilled in speech?" Exodus 6:12 (NASB)

6. But when Pharaoh saw that there was relief, he hardened his heart and would not **listen** to Moses and Aaron, just as the Lord had said. Exodus 8:15 (NIV)

7. But the Lord hardened Pharaoh's heart and he would not **listen** to Moses and Aaron, just as the Lord had said to Moses. Exodus 9:12 (NIV)

8. Moses **listen**ed to his father-in-law and did everything he said. Exodus 18:24 (NIV)

9. Pay attention to him and **listen** to what he says. Do not rebel against him; he will not forgive your rebellion, since my Name is in him. Exodus 23:21 (NIV)

10. If after all this you will not **listen** to me, I will punish you for your sins seven times over. Leviticus 26:18 (NIV)

11. He said, "**Listen** to my words: When there is a prophet among you, I, the Lord, reveal myself to them in visions, I speak to them in dreams." Numbers 12:6 (NIV)

12. So, I told you, but you would not **listen**. You rebelled against the Lord's command and in your arrogance, you marched up into the hill country. Deuteronomy 1:43 (NIV)

13. Go near and **listen** to all that the Lord our God says. Then tell us whatever the Lord our God tells you. We will **listen** and obey. Deuteronomy 5:27 (NIV)

14. I feared the anger and wrath of the Lord, for he was angry enough with you to destroy you. But again, the Lord **listen**ed to me. Deuteronomy 9:19 (NIV)

15. The Blessing: if you **listen** obediently to the commandments of God, your God, which I command you today Deuteronomy 11:27 (MSG)

16. Then Joshua said to the Israelites, "Come here and **listen** to the words of the Lord your God." Joshua 3:9 (NCV)

17. I said to you, "I am the Lord your God; do not worship the gods of the Amorites, in whose land you live." But you have not **listen**ed to me. Judges 6:10 (NIV)

18. So, Boaz said to Ruth, "My daughter, **listen** to me. Don't go and glean in another field and don't go away from here. Stay here with the women who work for me." Ruth 2:8 (NIV)

19. The Lord came and stood there, calling as at the other times, "Samuel! Samuel!" Then Samuel said, "Speak, for your servant is **listen**ing." 1 Samuel 3:10 (NIV)

20. A wise woman called from the city, "**Listen! Listen!** Tell Joab to come here so I can speak to him." 2 Samuel 20:16 (NIV)

21. Here's what I want: Give me a God-**listen**ing heart so I can lead your people well, discerning the difference between good and evil. For who on their own is capable of leading your glorious people? 1 Kings 3:9 (MSG)

22. From all nations people came to **listen** to Solomon's wisdom, sent by all the kings of the world, who had heard of his wisdom. 1 Kings 4:34 (NIV)

23. Give me a God listening heart so I can lead your people well, discerning the difference between good *and* evil. for who on their own is capable of leading your glorious people? 1 Kings 3:9 (MSG)

24. Then Jehoahaz sought the Lord's favor, and the Lord **listen**ed to him, for he saw how severely the king of Aram was oppressing Israel. 2 Kings 13:4 (NIV)

25. King David rose to his feet and said, "**Listen** to me, my fellow Israelites, my people. I had it in my heart to build a house as a place of rest for the ark of the covenant of the Lord, for the footstool of our God, and I made plans to build it." 1 Chronicles 28:2 (NIV)

26. Now **listen** to me! Send back your fellow Israelites you have taken as prisoners, for the Lord's fierce anger rests on you. 2 Chronicles 28:11 (NIV)

27. So, we fasted and sought our God concerning this matter, and He listened to our entreaty. Ezra 8:23 (NAS)

28. He read it aloud from daybreak till noon as he faced the square before the Water Gate in the presence of the men, women and others who could understand, and all the people **listen**ed attentively to the Book of the Law. Nehemiah 8:3 (NIV)

29. **Listen** carefully to what I say; let my words ring in your ears. Job 13:17 (NIV)

30. People **listen**ed to me carefully and waited quietly for my advice. Job 29:21 (NCV)

31. Listen to my words, Job; pay attention to what I have to say. Job 33:31 (NLT)

32. In the morning, LORD, you hear my voice; in the morning, I lay my requests before you and wait expectantly. Psalm 5:3 (NIV)

33. **Listen**, daughter, and pay careful attention: Forget your people and your father's house. Psalm 45:10 (NIV)

34. **Listen**, my people, and I will warn you. Israel, if only you would obey me! Psalm 81:8 (ISV)

35. I will hear what God the LORD will speak: for he will speak peace unto his people, and to his saints: but let them not turn again to folly. Psalm 85:8 (KJV)

36. Let the wise **listen** and add to their learning, and let the discerning get guidance. Proverbs 1:5 (NIV)

37. But whoever **listen**s to me will dwell safely and will be secure from fear of evil. Proverbs 1:33 (MEV)

38. **Listen**, my son, accept what I say, and the years of your life will be many. Proverbs 4:10 (NIV)

39. **Listen** to advice and accept discipline, and at the end you will be counted among the wise. Proverbs 19:20 (NIV)

40. Like an earring of gold or an ornament of fine gold is the rebuke of a wise judge to a **listen**ing ear. Proverbs 25:12 (NIV)

41. It is better to heed the rebuke of a wise person than to **listen** to the song of fools. Ecclesiastes 7:5 (NIV)

42. **Listen**! My beloved! Look! Here he comes, leaping across the mountains, bounding over the hills. Song of Songs 2:8 (NIV)

43. **Listen** and hear my voice; pay attention and hear what I say. Isaiah 28:23 (NIV)

44. The eyes of those who see shall not be blinded, and the ears of those who hear shall **listen**. Isaiah 32:3 (MEV)

45. You have seen many things, but you pay no attention; your ears are open, but you do not **listen**. Isaiah 42:20 (NIV)

46. The Lord said to me, "Proclaim all these words in the towns of Judah and in the streets of Jerusalem: '**Listen** to the terms of this covenant and follow them.'" Jeremiah 11:6 (NIV)

47. "But if a nation will not **listen** to my message, I will pull it up completely and destroy it," says the Lord. Jeremiah 12:17 (NCV)

48. For twenty-three years—from the thirteenth year of Josiah son of Amon king of Judah until this very day—the Word of the Lord has come to me and I have spoken to you again and again, but you have not **listen**ed. Jeremiah 25:3 (NIV)

49. The Lord is righteous, yet I rebelled against his command. **Listen**, all you peoples; look on my suffering. My young men and young women have gone into exile. Lamentations 1:18 (NIV)

50. You must speak my words to them, whether they **listen** or fail to **listen**, for they are rebellious. Ezekiel 2:7 (NIV)

51. But the house of Israel will not be willing to listen to you, for they are not willing to listen to me: because all the house of Israel have a hard forehead and a stubborn heart. Ezekiel 3:7 (ESV)

52. Lord, **listen**! Lord, forgive! Lord, hear and act! For your sake, my God, do not delay, because your city and your people bear your Name. Daniel 9:19 (NIV)

53. Hear this, you priests! Pay attention, you Israelites! **Listen**, royal house! This judgment is against you: You have been a snare at Mizpah, a net spread out on Tabor. Hosea 5:1 (NIV)

54. Hear this, you elders; **listen**, all who live in the land. Has anything like this ever happened in your days or in the days of your ancestors? Joel 1:2 (NIV)

55. Away with the noise of your songs! I will not **listen** to the music of your harps. Amos 5:23 (NIV)

56. The vision of **Obadiah**. This is what the Sovereign Lord says about Edom— We have **hear**d a message from the Lord: An envoy was sent to the nations to say, "Rise, let us go against her for battle." Obadiah 1:1 (NIV)

57. He said: "In my distress I called to the Lord, and he answered me. From deep in the realm of the dead I called for help, and you **listen**ed to my cry." Jonah 2:2 (NIV)

58. **Listen** to what the Lord says: "Stand up, plead my case before the mountains; let the hills hear what you have to say." Micah 6:1 (NIV)

59. How long, Lord, must I call for help, but you do not **listen**? Or cry out to you, "Violence!" but you do not save? Habakkuk 1:2 (NIV)

60. Do not be like your ancestors, to whom the earlier prophets proclaimed: This is what the Lord Almighty says: "Turn from your evil ways and your evil

practices." But they would not **listen** or pay attention to me, declares the Lord. Zechariah 1:4 (NIV)

61.　So [this is what God-of-the-Angel-Armies said] if they won't **listen** to me, I won't **listen** to them. I scattered them to the four winds. They ended up strangers wherever they were. Their "promised land" became a vacant lot—weeds and tin cans and thistles. Not a sign of life. They turned a dreamland into a wasteland. Zechariah 7:13-14 (MSG)

62.　"If you do not **listen**, and if you do not resolve to honor my name," says the Lord Almighty, "I will send a curse on you, and I will curse your blessings. Yes, I have already cursed them, because you have not resolved to honor me." Malachi 2:2 (NIV)

63.　If anyone will not welcome you or **listen** to your words, leave that home or town and shake the dust off your feet. Matthew 10:14 (NIV)

64.　**Listen** then to what the parable of the sower means. Matthew 13:18 (NIV)

65.　Are you **listen**ing to this? Really **listen**ing? Mark 4:9 (MSG)

66.　Just then a light-radiant cloud enveloped them, and from deep in the cloud, a voice: "This is my Son, marked by my love. **Listen** to him." Mark 9:7 (MSG)

67.　The stony ground represents those who enjoy **listen**ing to sermons, but somehow the message never really gets through to them and doesn't take root and grow. They know the message is true, and sort of believe for a while; but when the hot winds of persecution blow, they lose interest. Luke 8:13 (TLB)

68. Therefore, consider carefully how you **listen**. Whoever has will be given more; whoever does not have, even what they think they have will be taken from them. Luke 8:18 (NIV)

69. He who **listen**s to you **listen**s to Me, he who rejects you rejects Me, and he who rejects Me rejects Him who sent Me. Luke 10:16 (MEV)

70. What you have said in the dark will be **heard** in the daylight, and what you have whispered in the ear in the inner rooms will be proclaimed from the roofs. Luke 12:3 (NIV)

71. And I solemnly declare that the time is coming, in fact, it is here, when the dead shall hear my voice—the voice of the Son of God—and those who **listen** shall live. John 5:25 (TLB)

72. We know that God does not **listen** to sinners. He **listen**s to the godly person who does his will. John 9:31 (NIV)

73. My sheep listen to my voice; I know them, and they follow me. John 10:27 (NLT)

74. And it shall come to pass, that every soul, which will not **hear** that prophet, shall be destroyed from among the people. Acts 3:23 (KJV)

75. After they had become silent, James answered, "Brothers, **listen** to me." Acts 15:13 (MEV)

76. Therefore, I want you to know that God's salvation has been sent to the Gentiles, and they will **listen**! Acts 28:28 (NIV)

77. For not the **hear**ers of the law are just before God, but the doers of the law shall be justified. Romans 2:13 (KJV)

78. So, then faith cometh by **hear**ing, and **hear**ing by the Word of God. Romans 10:17 (KJV)

79. In the Law it is written: "With other tongues and through the lips of foreigners I will speak to this people, but even then, they will not **listen** to me, says the Lord." 1 Corinthians 14:21 (NIV)

80. How that he was caught up into paradise, and **hear**d unspeakable words, which it is not lawful for a man to utter. 2 Corinthians 12:4 (KJV)

81. So then, does God give you the Spirit and work miracles among you by your doing the works of the law? Or is it by believing what you **hear**d. Galatians 3:5 (CSB)

82. Do not let any unwholesome talk come out of your mouths, but only what is helpful for building others up according to their needs, that it may benefit those who **listen**. Ephesians 4:29 (NIV)

83. Just one thing: As citizens of heaven, live your life worthy of the gospel of Christ. Then, whether I come and see you or am absent, I will **hear** about you that you are standing firm in one spirit, in one accord, contending together for the faith of the gospel. Philippians 1:27 (CSB)

84. Whatever you have learned or received or heard from me or seen in me—put it into practice. And the God of peace will be with you. Philippians 4:9 (NIV)

85. For we have **hear**d of your faith in Christ Jesus and of the love you have for all the saints. Colossians 1:4 (CSB)

86. This is why we constantly thank God, because when you received the Word of God that you **hear**d from us, you welcomed it not as a human message, but as it

truly is, the Word of God, which also works effectively in you who believe. 1 Thessalonians 2:13 (CSB)

87. For we **hear** that there are some among you who are idle. They are not busy but busybodies. 2 Thessalonians 3:11 (CSB)

88. Take heed unto thyself, and unto the doctrine; continue in them: for in doing this thou shalt both save thyself, and them that **hear** thee. 1 Timothy 4:16 (KJV)

89. For the time will come when people will not tolerate sound doctrine, but according to their own desires, will multiply teachers for themselves because they have an itch to **hear** what they want to **hear**. 2 Timothy 4:3 (NIV)

90. **Hear**ing of thy love and faith, which thou hast toward the Lord Jesus, and toward all saints. Philemon 1:5 (KJV)

91. For this reason, we must pay attention all the more to what we have **hear**d, so that we will not drift away. Hebrews 2:1 (CSB)

92. My dear brothers and sisters, take note of this: Everyone should be quick to **listen**, slow to speak and slow to become angry. James 1:19 (NIV)

93. Do not merely **listen** to the word, and so deceive yourselves. Do what it says. James 1:22 (NIV)

94. The Lord watches over everyone who obeys him, and he **listen**s to their prayers. But he opposes everyone who does evil. 1 Peter 3:12 (CEV)

95. And this voice which came from heaven we **hear**d, when we were with him in the holy mount. 2 Peter 1:18 (KJV)

96. We are from God, and whoever knows God **listen**s to us; but whoever is not from God does not **listen** to us. This is how we recognize the Spirit of truth and the spirit of falsehood. 1 John 4:6 (NIV)

97. This is love: that we walk according to his commands. This is the command as you have **hear**d it from the beginning: that you walk in love. 2 John 1:6 (CSB)

98. I have no greater joy than this: to **hear** that my children are walking in truth. 3 John 1:4 (CSB)

99. If you have ears, **listen** to what the Spirit says to the churches. I will let everyone who wins the victory eat from the life-giving tree in God's wonderful garden. Revelation 2:7 (CEV)

100. If you have ears, then **listen!** Revelation 13:9 (CEV)

67003046R00096

Made in the USA
Columbia, SC
27 July 2019